dc
6'24

Celestial Navigation

Celestial Navigation

A PRACTICAL GUIDE TO KNOWING WHERE YOU ARE

DAVID BERSON

Seahorse Publishing

Copyright © 2018 by Dave Berson
Foreword copyright © 2017 by Tim Queeney
Foreword copyright © 2017 by Eben Whitcomb

Seahorse Publishing books may be purchased in bulk at special discounts for sales promotion, corporate gifts, fund-raising, or educational purposes. Special editions can also be created to specifications. For details, contact the Special Sales Department, Skyhorse Publishing, 307 West 36th Street, 11th Floor, New York, NY 10018 or info@skyhorsepublishing.com.

Seahorse® and Seahorse Publishing® are registered trademarks of Skyhorse Publishing, Inc.®, a Delaware corporation.

Visit our website at www.skyhorsepublishing.com.

10 9 8 7 6 5 4 3 2

Library of Congress Cataloging-in-Publication Data is available on file.

Cover design by Tom Lau
Cover photo credit: *Eight Bells* (1886) by Winslow Homer, courtesy of the Addison Gallery of American Art

Print ISBN: 9781944824020
Ebook ISBN: 9781944824037

Printed in China

For George and Sophie, who showed me the way

Contents

Foreword

by Tim Queeney

Celestial navigation is a wonderfully simple and reliable method for finding your way across the sea. No high tech gear, no electronics, and no electricity at all is required. It's that basic—a throwback to an age of canvas sails and ships built of timber.

Most people have not even seen the device most frequently used in celestial navigation: it's called a sextant. It's a cool-looking instrument with a handle and some mirrors and a sliding arm on a scale that you can learn to use after some practice. Dead simple, really.

A sextant . . . oh, and a nautical almanac also comes in handy. The almanac is a book with rows and columns of dates and numbers. It's used to find the position of the sun, moon, planets, and stars. These are what you point the sextant at. So that's it, a sextant and an almanac are all you need to engage in the art of celestial navigation.

Plus, of course, sight reduction tables also come in handy. These are more books with rows and columns of tiny numbers (maybe use a ruler to keep your place). The sight reduction tables are how you start with a sight of the sun, for example, and end up with a Line of Position. This isn't the same as a latitude/longitude fix. Anyway, the key thing to remember is that this simple navigation technique only requires a sextant, nautical almanac, and sight reduction tables.

You'll need a watch, too. To get your Line of Position of the sun, you need to know the time you took the sight, down to the exact second. But watches are so accurate these days and inexpensive, too. So a sextant, almanac, sight tables, and a watch and you're good to go.

You might also want some plotting sheets, dividers, parallel rules, pencils, erasers, triangles, a drawing compass, and a few more things. Along with some time to practice your sextant work and plotting and familiarity with dead reckoning and star identification and a few more things too tangential to address here.

Simple.

Wait, you're saying that's not so simple? That a GPS (global positioning system) gives you a position and so why carry around all that stuff and have to practice with it too?

It's a fair point.

Utilizing a GPS is way easier and quicker and it is omnipresent. Why bother with anything else? The reasons to learn celestial navigation really boil down to two:

1. A backup system in case your electrical items fail and all your extra batteries go dead (okay, unlikely, but it could happen). Which brings us to reason number 2 (which really should be reason number 1, I guess).

2. You learn celestial navigation for the same reason you learn to ski, play video games, or sail, for that matter: because it's fun and rewarding.

There's nothing quite like that feeling of self-sufficiency and accomplishment (except perhaps Nordic skiing across Antarctica in the austral winter eating only pemmican) when an island swims up on the horizon exactly when and where you said it would. Your shipmates will be amazed that all you used to navigate the passage was a sextant, almanac, sight reduction tables, plotting sheet, parallel rules—well, you get the idea.

—Tim Queeney
Editor, *Ocean Navigator* magazine

Foreword

by Eben Whitcomb

For several thousand years celestial navigation has developed to help accurately determine a ship's position whilst on the open sea. This began with efforts to fix the altitude of celestial bodies, principally the sun and polaris, for a value of latitude. The value of longitude, on the other hand, eluded navigators for ages. But in 1714, the British Parliament passed the Longitude Act, which awarded various prizes for practical methods of determining longitude. It took considerable time before the largest prize was awarded to Mr. John Harrison (deceased by that time), who had invented a chronometer capable of keeping accurate time at sea (a pendulum clock will not work on a ship). Another big winner calculated the time for a voyage from England to Jamaica to an accuracy of less than ten seconds. Unfortunately, the cost of such an instrument was so great as to be unaffordable by most mariners.

In 1830, Captain Robert FitzRoy outfitted the rebuilt *Beagle* for a four-year voyage of circumnavigation (with

Charles Darwin aboard as naturalist). The voyage's purpose was to map the exact latitude and longitude of islands and continents along his route. The Admiralty outfitted the ship with sixteen chronometers and Captain FitzRoy purchased an additional six at his own expense! But even with this accurate time, it was necessary to perform complicated mathematics to reach the end result.

We have come a long way since then and most of us have been seduced by today's electronic navigation. This tends to leave many with the impression that to work out your geographic position back in the day was extremely difficult, requiring a lot of calculations and new definitions. Having taught sailors and would-be sailors celestial navigation for thirty-plus years, David Berson has done us a great service in creating a step-by-step procedure that is simple, straightforward, and easy to learn.

And when learning celestial navigation, you do not have to be a mathematician or an astronomer, and yet you will feel confident that you will reach your destination when you are on that open ocean voyage. Once started there are many refinements that may be added, if you wish, but with the basics David has presented in this volume, you will enjoy the satisfaction it gives when you launch your vessel from the dock and go to sea with confidence (and it also will supply a great subject for small talk at cocktail parties).

—Captain Eben Whitcomb

Introduction

There are so many misconceptions surrounding the learning and practice of celestial navigation that it is no surprise that many are loathe to tackle the subject. They believe, incorrectly, that they have to be some sort of wizard with numbers before they can be proficient. It is true that once, a long time ago, in a faraway place, mariners had to be familiar with spherical trigonometry and all sorts of other mathematical exotica in order to calculate position. But no longer. All that changed during the Second World War when thousands of young men were tasked to learn celestial navigation in ninety days so they could take command of vessels.

Sight reduction tables were simplified and knowledge of spherical trigonometry was no longer necessary. The same process took place amongst young pilots who needed to learn how to navigate as they flew planes across the Atlantic and Pacific oceans. The sight reduction tables we now use (HO249) were specifically designed for these airborne navigators. So the myth of having to be an accomplished whiz at numbers in order to navigate is just that—a myth. True, we still have to know how to add and subtract, but even for those of us who slept through school, this is not that great a challenge.

The other misconception about celestial navigation is that it is outmoded and has no value. Certainly with the proliferation of GPS and its amazing accuracy, there is a point to be made. But GPS relies on satellites and electronic hocus pocus that is neither easy nor inexpensive to troubleshoot. Celestial navigation on the other hand is virtually foolproof once you comprehend the basics, and so important that the US Navy has reinstated teaching it to its cadets at the Naval Academy. I am not suggesting that you choose one method over another. You can have a reliable, accurate GPS aboard a ship and still practice celestial navigation. Actually, GPS will make you a better student of the celestial because it acts as a master teacher.

Another argument against learning celestial navigation is that it just takes too much time. This is a fair point. It is easier and faster to push a button. But so what? Most yachts are moving at 10 mph or less, so there's plenty of time at sea to sleep, eat, stand watch, and even practice celestial navigation. It just means you'll have less time to read trashy novels.

Many of these misconceptions, ironically, have been promoted by those who actually practice celestial navigation, especially those who practiced it during the Second World War. Navigation was kept as much a mystery as possible to the rest of the crew. This was essentially because navigators didn't want anyone else to know what a cushy job it was. Better to make it seem obtuse and complicated so the navigators could be left alone. In my own experience, I have found this to be true. When I first began ocean sailing, navigators either deliberately, or because they didn't know any better, obfuscated and confused me so much that I actually gave up trying to learn. But I did eventually learn because I soon found out that despite my limited strength and sailing skills, I could always find a paying job as a navigator. When I began teaching, I endeavored to cut through all the unnecessary information so I could get to the core of the matter. I would do my best to simplify, always so that the student could understand the theory and the process without being obstructed by too much mumbo jumbo.

I have written this book for those of us who want to learn without too much confusion. It is for students who, like myself, always sat in the back of the classroom, who were smart but not prodigies, who found it more engaging to stare out the window than listen to the teacher, for those of us who still have to count on our fingers and for whom learning is sometimes a pain in the neck. Trust me when I tell you that I am one of those people. But what will make this endeavor worth your while is that the results are so astounding, the pleasure accrued so great, I am almost willing to say that learning celestial navigation can be a transforming experience. For me, it opened up the world of the night sky, the movements of celestial objects, and a greater respect for previous generations who spent their lives attempting to unravel the mysteries of the universe. Celestial navigation is a great voyage of discovery, relatively inexpensive to get into, that will provide years of quiet enjoyment. I guarantee it.

Woody Guthrie once remarked about a cup of coffee that it promises much but delivers little. This may be true about coffee but not about this book. Herein I make very modest promises on which I will deliver. I promise that if you tag along on this journey, by the end of these pages you will have both the self-confidence and the knowledge to navigate by the sun. Of course, your skills will be rudimentary, but in the process of doing—as in anything else we endeavor to learn—the more we do, the more proficient we become. And hopefully the information presented will inspire you to read more deeply on this most fascinating subject.

The theory and practice of celestial navigation has been written about in countless books over many years. What I am attempting here is to distill what I have learned so that the reader won't get lost or waylaid. This is my take, if you will, on what the learning and doing of celestial navigation is all about. I have a lot of experience practicing and teaching this subject and I like to think I understand it, but my style may not work for all. I'm giving it my best shot, and at worst, you will have to read other books before you understand the subject. I have full bookshelves devoted to celestial navigation. As with everything, some of these are better than others.

Writers such as Nathaniel Bowditch, George W. Mixter, Mary Blewett, and Francis Wright have said all of this before in their own ways. Friends and teachers such as the late Dr. Fred Hess, Captain Eben Whitcomb, Greg Walsh, Ken Hamilton, Steve Burzon, and Nick van Nes have all contributed to my understanding. A mention should also be made of the influence that the New York Hayden Planetarium had on my learning. As a young boy, my father would take me to the Planetarium every Saturday morning for lectures in the sky dome on astronomy. My first class in celestial navigation was given to me many years later by the legendary Dr. Fred Hess, who had complete mastery of the subject. When Dr. Hess retired, I was fortunate enough to be asked, along with a few others, to attempt to carry on what he had begun. No one, of course, could fill Dr. Hess's shoes, but it was a great thrill for me nevertheless.

Thanks to Meg Bennett, who transcribed my notes, drew the fabulous diagrams, and without whom this book would not exist, and to *Ocean Navigator* magazine for giving me the opportunity to hone my skills as both writer and teacher. Finally, a great debt to my editor, Jay Cassell, who is no quitter.

Purpose

Celestial navigation in itself is not confusing. Simply put, it is the use of stars, planets, the sun, and the moon as a means of finding an observer's position. With the use of a sextant, which is really nothing more than a very sophisticated protractor, and some math tables evolved over many generations, we are able to calculate exactly where we are in relation to celestial objects.

My own interest in celestial navigation began with a painting. It's the one on the cover of this book, in fact. It shows two men dressed in oilskins on a deck of a sailing ship. The sea is running and the sky, all grays except for an opening of blue where the sun may be. The men are holding in their hands objects—octants, actually—and one is taking a sight of the sun while the other is staring intently at the numbers on the arc of the octant. The painting, by Winslow Homer, is called *Eight Bells* (1886) and depicts the marking of the moment of astronomical noon when mariners take a sight of the sun as it crosses their meridian. It's an effective and simple method of finding latitude, as valid now as it was one hundred fifty years ago. One can almost hear the striking of the ship's bell. *Ding-ding. Ding-ding. Ding-ding. Ding-ding.*

Of course, I didn't know all of this when, as a young boy, my father took me to the museum to stand before the picture. He wasn't sure what the sailors were doing, but something in that painting resonated with me. The idea of adventures beyond the streets of my native Bronx, the pull of an imaginary dream. Think Jack London or Robert Louis Stevenson.

Understanding what those sailors were doing, and why, has become a strong intellectual pursuit in my life. The book you are holding in your hand attempts to answer those questions and will teach you how you too can learn to use a sextant to fix your position at sea, perhaps not as accurately as GPS, but accurately enough to navigate with confidence. Armed with some inexpensive tables, an up-to-date nautical almanac, dividers, parallel rules, and with little or no math skills beyond the basics, you can successfully navigate using the sun. Even though celestial navigation will not make you richer, smarter, or a better person, it may possibly scratch an intellectual itch that you weren't even aware of, while yielding great satisfaction and a greater understanding of the universe we inhabit.

With a subject as dense as celestial navigation, it is tricky to know where to begin: the celestial sphere? the math? the involved assumptions? As for me, I have chosen to enter this pool of knowledge at the proverbial children's end where I can stand up and touch bottom with some basic concepts.

Before continuing, a word of caution. I have made certain assumptions about the skill level of the reader. I have assumed that the reader is already familiar with the basic aspects of coastal navigation, plotting, how to maintain a DR (deduced reckoning), how to lay out a course, and how to advance a Line of Position. If you are not knowledgeable about these aspects of navigation, I would suggest you become comfortable with them before getting into celestial navigation. There are copious amounts of information already written about these topics, most especially in *Chapman Piloting & Seamanship*. To delve into a discussion about celestial navigation without some basic building blocks of information would be both frustrating and futile. Even with this prior knowledge, you still will be challenged. Someone I once taught described the process of learning celestial navigation as a "great big scavenger hunt." There is a lot of information to absorb and it is easy to get lost in the process while learning. Consult as often as possible the flow chart at the back of the book. It will be of great help when the numbers begin to pile up.

Let's start:

We are standing beneath a flagpole. Don't ask why, we just are. If we look straight up, the top of the flagpole is directly overhead. If we had a protractor in our hand, we could measure the angle to the top of the flagpole. It would be 90°. Overhead is measured at 90° with the horizon. This is also called, for the sake of celestial speak, "the Zenith." Zenith means directly overhead, or measuring 90° from the observer. Now let's imagine we walk twenty-five steps from the flagpole. It doesn't matter in which direction. Using our protractor we could measure the angle from where we stand to the top of the flagpole. It would be less than 90°. Let's say for argument's sake that it is 70°. And if we walked around the flagpole at a distance of twenty-five steps, in any direction, the angle of the protractor would still read 70°. If we walk completely around the flagpole dragging a stick and making a circle, everywhere on that circle at a distance of twenty-five steps, the protractor would read the same angle of 70°.

So here are two things to know: The first is that the circle we have just drawn has a fancy name in celestial speak. It is called the Circle of Position. The second thing we have just learned is that as one moves further away from the flagpole (or, the zenith), the lower the number recorded on the protractor becomes; thus, the distance from zenith can be measured by an angular measurement. The farther away a point is from the zenith, the smaller the angle from the observer to the top of the flagpole.

Let's continue on our circular walk, but now let's move fifty steps from the flagpole. The angle on the protractor will decrease to say 50°. The angle decreases as we move farther away. We now have a second Circle of Position and everywhere on that circle the protractor measures 50°. It is clear that the closer we are to the flagpole, the greater the angle. The farther we move away from the flagpole, increasing our distance, the smaller the angle becomes. This is important to absorb: There is a direct relationship between the angle of the observer and the distance between the observer and the observed object. If we are fifty feet away from the flagpole, we could walk around it and the angle would be the same at every point in the

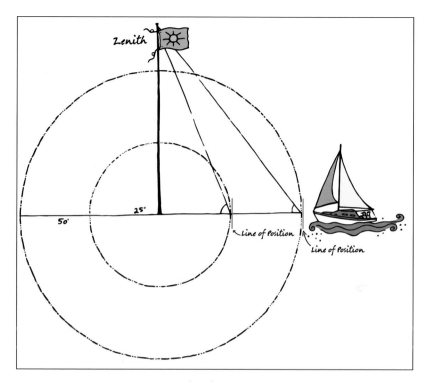

Circle of Position.

circle. The same would hold true if we are a hundred feet away or two hundred feet, etc.

If we had a compass, as well as our protractor, we could use the compass to find our direction, or bearing, to the flagpole. Then we would know exactly where we are on that Circle of Position. If the flagpole is bearing 270° and we are at an angular measured distance of 40°, we could only be at one place on that circle. Now let's take a breath and move this discussion to the next step. We are, after all, not interested in measuring our position relative to a flagpole. In coastal navigation, this is a valid technique, as we can see the latitude and longitude from looking at the chart (in other words, the position of the flagpole). We can find where we are relative to this known position by using a rangefinder with a compass. But as celestial navigators, we are measuring our distance and bearing not from a flagpole but from the sun. So how does that work?

Suppose, instead of a flagpole on Earth, we have a flagpole extending from the center of the earth to the sun. It's a mighty long flagpole indeed, but indulge me for a moment. Where that flagpole intersects the surface of the earth is called the sun's Geographical Position, or GP. It could be thousands of miles away, but we could still find out where we are in relation to it by measuring our distance and bearing from it. Instead of using a protractor, we are now using a sextant and we measure our angular distance from the sun's GP. If we know the exact location of that Geographical Position, and its direction or bearing, we can find out where

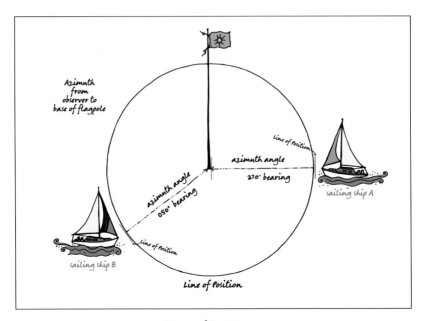

Line of Position.

we are in relation to it on our Circle of Position. That is the essence of celestial navigation.

I know what you're saying: "But we don't know the Geographical Position of the sun." Correction, yes, we do. We know the GP not only of the sun but also of four planets, fifty-seven stars, and the moon for every second, minute, hour, and day of every year. Instead of being referred to as latitude and longitude, as position on the earth is measured, the position of the GP of the celestial object is referred to as declination and Greenwich Hour Angle (GHA). But don't be confused: declination and Greenwich Hour Angle have a great deal in common with latitude and longitude; they are terms that apply to celestial objects more at home in the imaginary celestial sphere than on Earth. Not to worry, though. We can bring them to Earth, where we live.

With the help of the Nautical Almanac, which is really nothing more than a celestial timetable, we can find the coordinates of the declination and GHA. Then, using our sextant to measure the angular distance from us to the GP of the sun, we can find out where we are in relation to that fixed known object. Of course, this explanation doesn't take into account how this is done using spherical trigonometry and all kinds of other mathematical magic, which we don't need to know. Better minds than mine have already done all the hard work for us and tabulated the answers in sight reduction tables. If we could learn to use those tables, by no means that difficult, we can do celestial navigation.

I will prove that what I just said is true. Now of course, with circles of position that might be thousands of miles

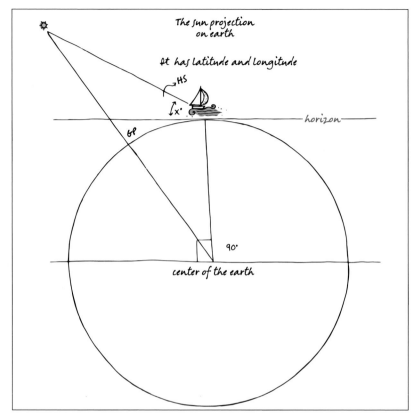

Sun Projection on the Earth.

in diameter we need to simplify the process so that we can get accurate results without having to draw humongous circles. Since we could only be at one point on a Circle of Position and since that circle is so large, we are actually on a very small segment of that circle and we all remember—don't we?—that a circle is mathematically a polygon with an infinite number of sides. We are on a segment of this huge circle represented as a straight line called a Line of Position (LOP). (See diagram on page 6.)

We know basically where we are at the time of our observations of the sun because we've been keeping a deduced reckoning (DR) of where our boat has been since we've left the dock. We know we are traveling at a certain speed on a certain course. We know that two hours after leaving the dock, we are at an approximate location based on our speed and the direction we've been traveling. So we always have an idea of where we have been. It isn't exact, but it's good enough for our purposes. As a result, we know where we are in terms of bearing in relation to the GP of the sun. When we measure our angular distance we know we are somewhere on the Circle of Position, on a small segment of it known as the LOP, or Line of Position. True, there are lots of bells and whistles in between. But they are not too difficult to master. Just always remember that it's all about where we are in relation to the GP of the celestial object as it extends from the sun through the center of the earth. George Mixter aptly referred to this concept as "lighthouses in the sky."

The Concept of the Celestial Sphere

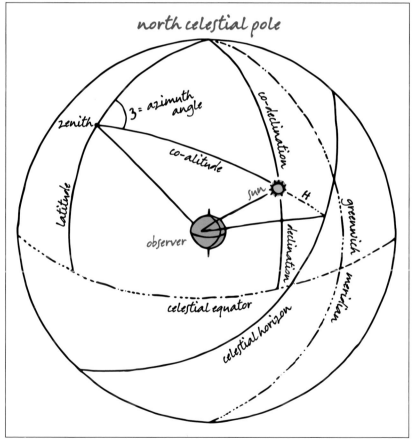

The Celestial Sphere.

The Greeks had it right when they would look at the night sky believing that everything seemed to be moving in a westerly direction. The stars in their regular places, the planets moving hither and yon, it looked to them—as it does to us now—that everything is spinning and moving around us. Of course, we know this isn't true. We know that we do not live in a geocentric world. The earth is not the center of the universe. We actually live in a heliocentric world where the sun is the center of our solar system. But it does appear—and for the sake of celestial navigation we hold this to be true—that the stars, planets, moon, and sun are fixed on a sphere at an infinite distance from the earth known as the celestial sphere. The appearance of the celestial sphere moving in a westerly direction is based on the fact that the earth—even though we can't feel it—is rotating in an easterly direction at about 900 miles an hour. So one of the first things we have to do when looking at the stars at night and the sun at day is to forget about Copernicus and Galileo, and revert to a more primitive and egocentric state of mind where we are at the center of the universe.

Necessary Books: *Nautical Almanac*

Science and magic meet in the *Nautical Almanac*. Published annually, it appears as interesting as an actuarial table, just a collection of numbers, but it is so much more. The *Nautical Almanac* is nothing less than a compilation of up-to-date information concerning the position (declination and GHA) of fifty-seven navigational stars, the sun, the moon, and four planets. The concept of a nautical almanac dates back to 1200 BC. The present iteration, compiled by both the US Naval Observatory and the British Hydrographic Office and available for less than $30, is a treasure trove of information that yields to the layperson without too much difficulty. It is true that it is a book filled with numbers that look threatening and obscure to those who have not been taught to understand its beauty and simplicity. Open any page and you may find yourself aghast at the endless rows of numbers. It's enough to make all us arithmophobic folks anxious, yet there is logic and simplicity to those numbers and the book is a wealth of information that is easy to decipher. And the amount of information is incredible.

The *Nautical Almanac* gives the reader the position of the sun and other navigational celestial objects for every second. This is equivalent to giving the GP of the celestial bodies as they seemingly move through the heavens. To reiterate: The GP of the sun is an exact spot on the surface of the earth where, if the sun were to be scrunched up into a little ball and thrown to the center of the earth, it would pass at a precise moment of time. That positon on the surface of the earth can be measured by latitude and longitude. In the celestial sphere it is measured by declination and GHA (Greenwich Hour Angle). If we know a position, in this case the GP of the sun, as measured by declination and GHA, we can measure where we are in relation to a known spot. So, essentially, celestial navigation is finding the GP of the sun and then calculating where we are in relation to that known position.

Allow me to digress for a moment. The origins of the nautical almanac began with the ancient Chinese and the culture of Mesopotamia. Ancient seers—they weren't called astronomers then—spent their lives observing the night sky, seeking patterns so that order could be divined from the seeming chaos. The movement of the stars was important to understanding the crop cycle. The observed world seemed to be working on a regular cycle and soon these seers were able to associate the rising and setting of certain stars with the natural events occurring on land. These high priests understood, without knowing how or why, a relationship between the appearance of certain stars and the change of seasons. Over generations they began calibrating the position of those stars when they appeared with the planting or harvest season. None of this happened overnight; it was a long process and every ancient culture performed the same quest.

The order that was observed in the heavens was made relevant to the order that we wished to create on Earth. The Babylonians kept their records on clay tablets, marking the passage of certain stars and the movement of planets—and this entire process was gone over and over again through thousands of years, evolved and refined; the modern version of all this is contained in the *Nautical Almanac*.

The modern almanac was first published in England in 1766. The United States was slow to follow and didn't produce its first nautical almanac until 1852. It wasn't until 1934 that the present format of the *Nautical Almanac* took shape when the GHA for sun, moon, and planets was introduced and the Sidereal Hour Angle (SHA) for the stars was introduced. There is also an air almanac that is published and is slightly different, but basically covers the

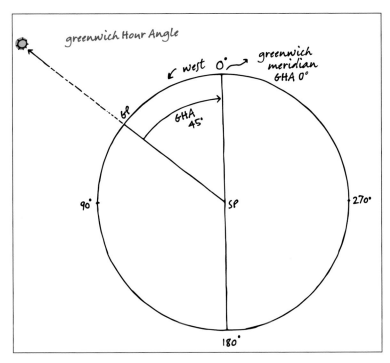

GHA from South Pole.

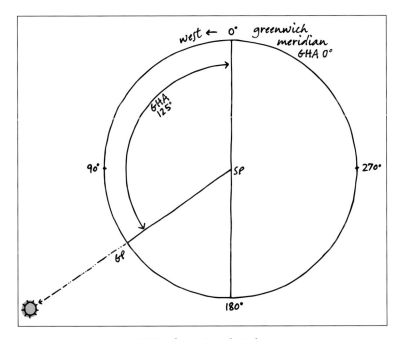

GHA from South Pole.

same information. We will, however, be dealing with the *Nautical Almanac.*

By providing GHA and declination of navigational bodies, a celestial navigator can find the exact position of that "flagpole" in the sky when taking a celestial observation. It is essential to remember that if a known object can be plotted with its latitude and longitude on the face of the earth—or its declination and its GHA in the celestial sphere—then the navigator can, by using some mathematical sleight of hand, find out where they are in relation to that object. We are attempting to find out where we are in relation to known objects. In this case, the objects aren't flagpoles or lighthouses as such, but celestial objects. With a watch and a sextant, the navigator can figure out where he or she is in relation to the celestial object.

Here is what we always know. We know basically where we are at the time of our celestial observations of the sun because we have been keeping a deduced reckoning (dead reckoning) of where we have been since casting off the dock. We know we are travelling at a certain speed on a specific course. We have a knot meter and a compass to verify this. We have an idea of where we are. Not precisely because we can't factor in steering error, or effects of the current, or the amount of leeway the vessel is making, but we do have an idea of where we might be. We label this on the chart as our DR position, our latitude and longitude. You must accept this as truth to continue. Even if you were set adrift in a raft and drifted about for days, you would still have known where you were before you started drifting. Hopefully.

Back to the Almanac

SUN / MOON

UT	SUN GHA	SUN Dec	MOON GHA	v	Dec	d	HP
d h	° ′	° ′	° ′	′	° ′	′	′
10 00	180 53.8	N17 28.6	285 59.5	8.4	S15 20.6	6.1	58.4
01	195 53.8	29.3	300 26.9	8.4	15 14.5	6.2	58.4
02	210 53.8	29.9	314 54.3	8.4	15 08.3	6.3	58.4
03	225 53.8	.. 30.6	329 21.7	8.5	15 02.0	6.4	58.4
04	240 53.9	31.3	343 49.2	8.4	14 55.6	6.5	58.4
05	255 53.9	31.9	358 16.6	8.5	14 49.1	6.6	58.5
06	270 53.9	N17 32.6	12 44.1	8.5	S14 42.5	6.7	58.5
07	285 53.9	33.2	27 11.6	8.5	14 35.8	6.7	58.5
08	300 54.0	33.9	41 39.1	8.5	14 29.1	6.9	58.5
S 09	315 54.0	.. 34.5	56 06.6	8.5	14 22.2	6.9	58.5
U 10	330 54.0	35.2	70 34.1	8.5	14 15.3	7.0	58.6
N 11	345 54.0	35.8	85 01.6	8.6	14 08.3	7.2	58.6
D 12	0 54.1	N17 36.5	99 29.2	8.5	S14 01.1	7.2	58.6
A 13	15 54.1	37.2	113 56.7	8.6	13 53.9	7.3	58.6
Y 14	30 54.1	37.8	128 24.3	8.6	13 46.6	7.3	58.6
15	45 54.1	.. 38.5	142 51.9	8.6	13 39.3	7.5	58.7
16	60 54.1	39.1	157 19.5	8.6	13 31.8	7.6	58.7
17	75 54.2	39.8	171 47.1	8.7	13 24.2	7.6	58.7
18	90 54.2	N17 40.4	186 14.8	8.6	S13 16.6	7.7	58.7
19	105 54.2	41.1	200 42.4	8.7	13 08.9	7.8	58.7
20	120 54.2	41.7	215 10.1	8.7	13 01.1	7.9	58.8
21	135 54.3	.. 42.4	229 37.8	8.7	12 53.2	8.0	58.8
22	150 54.3	43.0	244 05.5	8.7	12 45.2	8.0	58.8
23	165 54.3	43.7	258 33.2	8.7	12 37.2	8.1	58.8
11 00	180 54.3	N17 44.3	273 00.9	8.8	S12 29.1	8.2	58.8
01	195 54.3	45.0	287 28.7	8.7	12 20.9	8.3	58.8
02	210 54.4	45.6	301 56.4	8.8	12 12.6	8.4	58.9
03	225 54.4	.. 46.3	316 24.2	8.8	12 04.2	8.4	58.9
04	240 54.4	46.9	330 52.0	8.8	11 55.8	8.5	58.9
05	255 54.4	47.6	345 19.8	8.8	11 47.3	8.6	58.9
06	270 54.4	N17 48.2	359 47.6	8.9	S11 38.7	8.7	58.9
07	285 54.5	48.8	14 15.5	8.8	11 30.0	8.7	59.0
08	300 54.5	49.5	28 43.3	8.9	11 21.3	8.8	59.0
M 09	315 54.5	.. 50.1	43 11.2	8.9	11 12.5	8.9	59.0
O 10	330 54.5	50.8	57 39.1	8.9	11 03.6	8.9	59.0
N 11	345 54.5	51.4	72 07.0	8.9	10 54.7	9.1	59.0
D 12	0 54.5	N17 52.1	86 34.9	8.9	S10 45.6	9.0	59.0
A 13	15 54.6	52.7	101 02.8	8.9	10 36.6	9.2	59.1
Y 14	30 54.6	53.3	115 30.7	9.0	10 27.4	9.2	59.1
15	45 54.6	.. 54.0	129 58.7	9.0	10 18.2	9.3	59.1
16	60 54.6	54.6	144 26.7	8.9	10 08.9	9.4	59.1
17	75 54.6	55.3	158 54.6	9.0	9 59.5	9.4	59.1
18	90 54.6	N17 55.9	173 22.6	9.0	S 9 50.1	9.5	59.1
19	105 54.7	56.5	187 50.6	9.1	9 40.6	9.5	59.2
20	120 54.7	57.2	202 18.7	9.0	9 31.1	9.6	59.2
21	135 54.7	.. 57.8	216 46.7	9.0	9 21.5	9.7	59.2
22	150 54.7	58.5	231 14.7	9.1	9 11.8	9.7	59.2
23	165 54.7	59.1	245 42.8	9.1	9 02.1	9.8	59.2
12 00	180 54.7	N17 59.7	260 10.9	9.0	S 8 52.3	9.8	59.2
01	195 54.7	18 00.4	274 38.9	9.1	8 42.5	9.9	59.3
02	210 54.8	01.0	289 07.0	9.1	8 32.6	10.0	59.3
03	225 54.8	.. 01.6	303 35.1	9.1	8 22.6	10.0	59.3
04	240 54.8	02.3	318 03.2	9.2	8 12.6	10.1	59.3
05	255 54.8	02.9	332 31.4	9.1	8 02.5	10.1	59.3
06	270 54.8	N18 03.5	346 59.5	9.1	S 7 52.4	10.2	59.3
07	285 54.8	04.2	1 27.6	9.2	7 42.2	10.2	59.4
08	300 54.8	04.8	15 55.8	9.1	7 32.0	10.3	59.4
T 09	315 54.9	.. 05.4	30 23.9	9.2	7 21.7	10.3	59.4
U 10	330 54.9	06.1	44 52.1	9.2	7 11.4	10.4	59.4
E 11	345 54.9	06.7	59 20.3	9.2	7 01.0	10.4	59.4
S 12	0 54.9	N18 07.3	73 48.5	9.1	S 6 50.6	10.4	59.4
D 13	15 54.9	08.0	88 16.6	9.2	6 40.2	10.6	59.4
A 14	30 54.9	08.6	102 44.8	9.2	6 29.6	10.5	59.5
Y 15	45 54.9	.. 09.2	117 13.0	9.3	6 19.1	10.6	59.5
16	60 54.9	09.8	131 41.3	9.2	6 08.5	10.6	59.5
17	75 54.9	10.5	146 09.5	9.2	5 57.9	10.7	59.5
18	90 54.9	N18 11.1	160 37.7	9.2	S 5 47.2	10.7	59.5
19	105 55.0	11.7	175 05.9	9.3	5 36.5	10.8	59.5
20	120 55.0	12.3	189 34.2	9.2	5 25.7	10.8	59.5
21	135 55.0	.. 13.0	204 02.4	9.2	5 14.9	10.8	59.5
22	150 55.0	13.6	218 30.6	9.3	5 04.1	10.9	59.6
23	165 55.0	14.2	232 58.9	9.2	S 4 53.2	10.9	59.6
	SD 15.9	d 0.6	SD 16.0		16.1		16.2

Twilight / Sunrise / Moonrise

Lat.	Twilight Naut.	Twilight Civil	Sunrise	Moonrise 10	11	12	13
°	h m	h m	h m	h m	h m	h m	h m
N 72	□	□	□	02 49	02 42	02 36	02 30
N 70	////	////	01 26	02 15	02 20	02 23	02 24
68	////	////	02 10	01 51	02 04	02 13	02 20
66	////	00 31	02 39	01 31	01 50	02 04	02 15
64	////	01 36	03 01	01 16	01 39	01 57	02 12
62	////	02 09	03 19	01 03	01 29	01 50	02 09
60	00 27	02 33	03 33	00 52	01 21	01 45	02 06
N 58	01 26	02 52	03 45	00 42	01 14	01 40	02 04
56	01 57	03 08	03 56	00 34	01 07	01 36	02 01
54	02 19	03 21	04 05	00 27	01 01	01 32	01 59
52	02 37	03 32	04 13	00 20	00 56	01 28	01 58
50	02 52	03 42	04 21	00 14	00 51	01 25	01 56
45	03 20	04 03	04 36	00 01	00 41	01 18	01 53
N 40	03 42	04 19	04 49	24 32	00 32	01 12	01 50
35	03 59	04 32	05 00	24 25	00 25	01 07	01 47
30	04 13	04 44	05 10	24 19	00 19	01 02	01 45
20	04 35	05 02	05 26	24 07	00 07	00 55	01 41
N 10	04 52	05 18	05 40	23 57	24 48	00 48	01 37
0	05 06	05 31	05 53	23 48	24 41	00 41	01 34
S 10	05 18	05 44	06 06	23 39	24 35	00 35	01 31
20	05 30	05 56	06 19	23 29	24 28	00 28	01 27
30	05 45	06 10	06 35	23 18	24 20	00 20	01 24
35	05 47	06 17	06 44	23 11	24 16	00 16	01 21
40	05 53	06 25	06 54	23 03	24 10	00 10	01 19
45	05 59	06 35	07 06	22 55	24 04	00 04	01 16
S 50	06 06	06 45	07 21	22 44	23 57	25 12	01 12
52	06 09	06 50	07 27	22 39	23 54	25 11	01 11
54	06 13	06 56	07 35	22 34	23 50	25 09	01 09
56	06 16	07 01	07 43	22 28	23 46	25 07	01 07
58	06 20	07 08	07 53	22 21	23 42	25 05	01 05
S 60	06 24	07 15	08 03	22 13	23 37	25 02	01 02

Sunset / Twilight / Moonset

Lat.	Sunset	Twilight Civil	Twilight Naut.	Moonset 10	11	12	13
°	h m	h m	h m	h m	h m	h m	h m
N 72	07 38	////	////		09 37	11 34	13 29
N 70	22 34	////	////	08 11	09 57	11 45	13 33
68	21 46	////	////	08 35	10 13	11 53	13 36
66	21 16	23 51	////	08 53	10 25	12 01	13 38
64	20 54	22 22	////	09 08	10 35	12 07	13 40
62	20 36	21 47	////	09 20	10 44	12 12	13 41
60	20 22	21 22	23 52	09 30	10 52	12 16	13 43
N 58	20 09	21 03	22 31	09 40	10 58	12 20	13 44
56	19 58	20 47	21 59	09 47	11 04	12 24	13 45
54	19 49	20 33	21 36	09 55	11 09	12 27	13 46
52	19 41	20 22	21 18	10 01	11 14	12 30	13 47
50	19 33	20 12	21 03	10 07	11 18	12 33	13 48
45	19 17	19 51	20 34	10 19	11 27	12 38	13 50
N 40	19 04	19 34	20 12	10 29	11 35	12 43	13 52
35	18 53	19 21	19 55	10 38	11 42	12 47	13 53
30	18 44	19 10	19 41	10 45	11 47	12 50	13 54
20	18 27	18 51	19 18	10 58	11 57	12 56	13 56
N 10	18 13	18 35	19 01	11 09	12 06	13 02	13 58
0	18 00	18 22	18 47	11 20	12 14	13 07	13 59
S 10	17 47	18 09	18 34	11 31	12 21	13 11	14 01
20	17 33	17 56	18 23	11 42	12 30	13 17	14 02
30	17 17	17 43	18 11	11 54	12 39	13 22	14 04
35	17 08	17 35	18 06	12 02	12 45	13 26	14 05
40	16 58	17 27	18 00	12 10	12 51	13 29	14 06
45	16 48	17 18	17 53	12 20	12 58	13 34	14 08
S 50	16 32	17 07	17 46	12 31	13 07	13 39	14 09
52	16 25	17 02	17 43	12 36	13 11	13 41	14 10
54	16 17	16 57	17 39	12 42	13 15	13 44	14 11
56	16 09	16 51	17 36	12 49	13 20	13 47	14 11
58	15 59	16 44	17 32	12 56	13 25	13 50	14 12
S 60	15 49	16 37	17 28	13 05	13 31	13 53	14 13

SUN and MOON

Day	SUN Eqn. of Time 00h	SUN Eqn. of Time 12h	SUN Mer. Pass.	MOON Mer. Pass. Upper	MOON Mer. Pass. Lower	Age	Phase
d	m s	m s	h m	h m	h m	d %	
10	03 35	03 36	11 56	05 07	17 34	22 61	
11	03 37	03 38	11 56	06 01	18 27	23 49	
12	03 39	03 40	11 56	06 54	19 20	24 38	

On May 10, 2015, at 1500 hours Greenwich Mean Time (GMT), or Universal Time (UT) as it is referred to in the *Nautical Almanac*, we want to know the GP of the sun—in other words, where the sun would be if it fell to the center of the earth. One thing to know is that time in the *Nautical Almanac* for GHA and declination is always given as the time on the Greenwich meridian. We will discuss time a bit later on, but keep in mind that at sea, the navigator always has an accurate timepiece set to GMT.

The included section of the *Sun Daily* pages indicates that at 1500 hours GMT, the GHA, or longitude, if you will allow, of the sun is 45°54.1' and the declination (or Dec., as it is abbreviated) or latitude is N 17°38.5'. If we had a map of Earth, we could put the GP of the sun on it. It would be in the Atlantic Ocean east of South America.

One hour later, at 1600 GMT, we see that the GP of the sun has moved west, so that the GHA is 60°54.1' and the declination is N 17°39.1'.

At 1700 GMT, the GHA of the sun is now at 75°54.2' and the declination is at N 17°39.8'.

Let's see what we have just learned. The first thing is recognizing that the GHA (longitude, if you will) is changing much faster than the declination (latitude) of the sun. This will always be the case. You can pretty easily see that between 1500 hours and 1600 hours, the GHA of the sun moved about 15°. (See example from the *Nautical Almanac*, page 17.) This makes perfect sense because the earth is spinning at about 900 miles per hour; so, in an hour, the position of the sun has moved 15°. I found this by dividing 360° by 24 hours in a day. This comes out to 15°, which is what it appears the apparent sun moves every hour. The declination, on the other hand, changes very slowly. In the two hours from 1500 to 1700 GMT it has only changed from N 17°38.5' to N 17°39.8' or 1.3' A small change indeed. Actually, I know exactly how much the declination of the sun changes hourly because at the bottom of the sun pages is a small letter (d) that tells us that the sun is changing its declination at .6' every hour. By the way, at 1700 hours, the GP of the sun is in the Caribbean.

If you had a Mercator projection map of the earth, you could actually plot the movement of the sun by using the coordinates of declination and Greenwich Hour Angle found in the *Nautical Almanac*. Remember we are using the projection of the sun on the surface of the earth, and that the position of the sun is fixed by declination and Greenwich

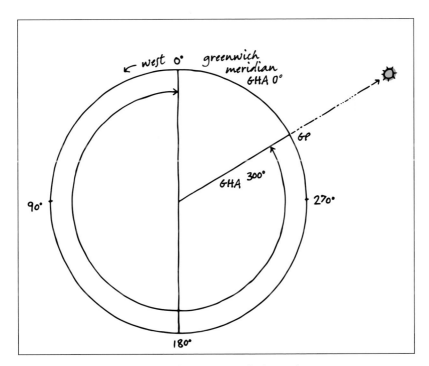

Greenwich Hour Angle (GHA).

Hour Angle, which are very similar to latitude and longitude. This is a very important concept to grasp, so it's crucial that you take this as slowly as you need to. In the celestial sphere, where the sun and the stars and moon and planets exist, positions are designated by the terms Declination and Greenwich Hour Angle. Declination is the same as latitude Earth. Always written first with a prefix designating whether it is North or South.

Reminder: Greenwich Hour Angle begins in the celestial sphere over the Greenwich meridian, or 0°, and is measured in a westerly direction through 360°. Thus, it differs from longitude in that longitude on the earth is measured from 0° to 180° east and west, whereas in the celestial sphere it appears, and correctly so, that the apparent sun is moving in a westerly direction each day every 24 hours. The sun doesn't get to 180° west longitude and then reverse direction.

Declination is similar to latitude. It begins at the Equator on the earth and on the celestial equator in the celestial sphere. It runs from 0° to 90° north and south. Again, it is important to remember that the art of navigation is measuring distance and bearing in relation to the Geographical Position of the celestial object. That GP of an object changes constantly and its changes are recorded in the *Nautical Almanac* under Declination and GHA. When doing celestial navigation, we are taking the celestial projections, declination, and GHA and bringing them to Earth.

Further, it is important to understand that if you know the position of an object as measured by latitude and longitude on the face of the earth, then you can find out where you are in relation to that known object. By using a sextant and sight reduction tables you can do just that. Instead of a known object on the surface of the earth, though, we are measuring our distance and bearing to the GP of the celestial object. Keep reflecting on this until it beings to make sense.

So, in short, with celestial navigation, we are not measuring our distance to the sun. Instead, we are using the sextant to measure our distance from the GP of the sun.

When we take an observation of the sun, we must time our sight so that we can find the exact GP of the sun at that moment. Very rarely, if indeed ever, is the time that we take our observation exactly on an hour, so it's important to know how to find the GP of the sun when there are minutes and seconds of time involved.

Let's stay on May 10 (please refer to chart on page 17) and say that we took an observation of the sun at 16:25:15 GMT. We want to find the exact GP of the sun at that time. Remember that everything appears to be moving in the celestial sphere and one minute of Earth time is equivalent to the apparent sun moving four nautical miles. So, we need to get this right because we want the exact GP of the sun at the moment of observation.

We are at sea and know that our last DR was at N 35°25' by W 68°19'. We can, using our sextant, measure the angular distance to the GP and then draw a Circle of Position of which the GP is the center.

In the example above, once again look under the left-hand column labeled "Sun GHA" for May 10 (page 17). Go down the column of UT (to the very left) to 1600 hours and write down the GHA and Declination. GHA at 16 hours GMT is 60°54.1'. The declination is N 17°39.1'. It is essential to make certain that you mark the degrees, minutes, and tenths of declination correctly. The sign of the declination is marked as either N or S at 00, 06, 012, or 018 hours. To make certain that you understand this, notice that the declination for 1700 hours is increasing by .6'. It is N 17°39.8'. The rate of hourly change for declination is labeled (d) at the bottom of the page.

Think about this: It should now make sense that the declination of the sun increases until the 21st of June, when we reach the summer solstice.

So now we have the GHA and declination for 1600 hours. That's great. But we took our time at 16:25:15 GMT. We need to find out how far the apparent sun has moved in 25 minutes and 15 seconds. We have already shown that the apparent sun is moving west at 15° every hour, so we can assume that the number we are looking for will be about half that. We don't have to guess, though, as there are tables in the rear of the *Nautical Almanac* that will give us the exact answer. Remember that the GP of the sun is the celestial equivalent of our flagpole. If we know the exact position of that flagpole, we can find out where we are in relation to it. (I realize that this may start sounding repetitive, but it is important, and thus worth repeating.)

At the end of the *Nautical Almanac* is the Corrections table (page 26 in this book). On the page that lists 25 minutes, you will see three columns labeled "Sun/Planets," "Aries," "Moon," and another three columns of "v" or d corrections. Don't get confused. Let's do one thing at a time.

Go down the column of 25' (arc) until you reach 15 seconds. Remember, our observation was at 16:25:15

GMT. Look under the "Sun/Planets" column and find the number 6°18.8'. This number means that in 25 minutes, 15 seconds the apparent sun has moved 6°18.8' in a westerly direction, which makes perfect sense since we have already established that the apparent sun is moving at about 15° an hour. It would make sense that in 25 minutes of time that the sun has moved almost one half that amount. Copy this number down, since it will be added to the GHA.

Now what about the declination? That too is changing—albeit much more slowly. But how much? Remember that declination in the celestial sphere corresponds to latitude on land. So in order to find the exact GP of the celestial object, we need to fix this position at the exact moment of our observation.

Go back to page 17 for the sun in the *Nautical Almanac* and notice at the bottom of the page, under the sun column, are two numbers. One is labeled SD, which stands for semi-diameter of the sun, a number that plays no importance in our present calculations. The other number, labeled d, is, in this case, .6'. This means that at this time of year the declination of the sun is changing at .6' minutes every hour—or sixth-tenths of a nautical mile per hour. This change needs to be calculated into the declination.

Back at the page in the *Nautical Almanac* that lists 25' of "Increments and Corrections," on page 26, look under the "v" or d columns. We look at the small-numbered left column and see that the d correction of .6' corresponds to a larger number .3'. This means that in 25 minutes of time, the declination of the sun has moved in a northerly direction .3'.

This makes sense, as the declination of the sun has moved half of the .6' correction. Now you may ask, do we add or subtract this from the declination? We see from observation of the Daily Pages that the declination is increasing every hour, so we add the 0.3 to the declination given at 1600 hours. Think about this for a moment so it makes sense. It is May, we are approaching the summer solstice on June 21, when the declination of the sun will be at its most northerly. It is logical then that the declination is increasing at this time of year. Of course, after the solstice, the declination of the sun will be again slowly moving south until the winter solstice, which takes place on December 21.

The d correction for the hourly change in declination at the bottom of the sun pages is not factored directly into our calculations. It is more like an arrow that is pointing to the exact correction that is added to or subtracted from the declination. We find the exact value of the d correction on the Increments table, and then factor that number, in the previous instance .3', into our calculations.

When written out, we have:

GHA at 16 hours,	60°54.1'
+ Increments and Corrections	+ 6°18.8'
GHA at time of sight	67°12.9'

Declination N 17°39.1 d correction at bottom of the page .6'
    which points to .3'
+ correction   .3'
Declination at 16:25:15 is N 17°39.4

2015 FEBRUARY 24, 25, 26 (TUES., WED., THURS.)   47

UT	SUN GHA	SUN Dec	MOON GHA	v	MOON Dec	d	HP
24 d h	° ′	° ′	° ′	′	° ′	′	′
00	176 40.5	S 9 39.5	111 25.0	8.9	N13 13.4	7.6	58.5
01	191 40.6	38.6	125 52.9	9.0	13 21.0	7.5	58.5
02	206 40.7	37.7	140 20.9	8.9	13 28.5	7.4	58.5
03	221 40.8 ..	36.8	154 48.8	8.9	13 35.9	7.4	58.4
04	236 40.9	35.9	169 16.7	9.0	13 43.3	7.2	58.4
05	251 41.0	34.9	183 44.7	9.0	13 50.5	7.2	58.3
T 06	266 41.1	S 9 34.0	198 12.7	9.0	N13 57.7	7.0	58.3
U 07	281 41.2	33.1	212 40.7	9.0	14 04.7	7.0	58.3
E 08	296 41.3	32.2	227 08.7	9.0	14 11.7	6.9	58.2
S 09	311 41.3 ..	31.2	241 36.7	9.0	14 18.6	6.8	58.2
D 10	326 41.4	30.3	256 04.7	9.0	14 25.4	6.7	58.2
A 11	341 41.5	29.4	270 32.7	9.1	14 32.1	6.6	58.1
Y 12	356 41.6	S 9 28.5	285 00.8	9.0	N14 38.7	6.5	58.1
13	11 41.7	27.6	299 28.8	9.1	14 45.2	6.5	58.0
14	26 41.8	26.6	313 56.9	9.1	14 51.7	6.3	58.0
15	41 41.9 ..	25.7	328 25.0	9.1	14 58.0	6.2	58.0
16	56 42.0	24.8	342 53.1	9.1	15 04.2	6.2	57.9
17	71 42.1	23.9	357 21.2	9.1	15 10.4	6.0	57.9
18	86 42.2	S 9 22.9	11 49.3	9.2	N15 16.4	6.0	57.8
19	101 42.3	22.0	26 17.5	9.1	15 22.4	5.8	57.8
20	116 42.4	21.1	40 45.6	9.2	15 28.2	5.8	57.8
21	131 42.4 ..	20.2	55 13.8	9.1	15 34.0	5.6	57.7
22	146 42.5	19.2	69 41.9	9.2	15 39.6	5.6	57.7
23	161 42.6	18.3	84 10.1	9.2	15 45.2	5.5	57.7
25 00	176 42.7	S 9 17.4	98 38.3	9.3	N15 50.7	5.3	57.6
01	191 42.8	16.5	113 06.6	9.2	15 56.0	5.3	57.6
02	206 42.9	15.5	127 34.8	9.3	16 01.3	5.2	57.5
03	221 43.0 ..	14.6	142 03.1	9.2	16 06.5	5.1	57.5
04	236 43.1	13.7	156 31.3	9.3	16 11.6	4.9	57.5
05	251 43.2	12.7	170 59.6	9.3	16 16.5	4.9	57.4
W 06	266 43.3	S 9 11.8	185 27.9	9.3	N16 21.4	4.8	57.4
E 07	281 43.4	10.9	199 56.2	9.4	16 26.2	4.7	57.4
D 08	296 43.5	10.0	214 24.6	9.3	16 30.9	4.6	57.3
N 09	311 43.6 ..	09.0	228 52.9	9.4	16 35.5	4.5	57.3
E 10	326 43.7	08.1	243 21.3	9.4	16 40.0	4.4	57.3
S 11	341 43.8	07.2	257 49.7	9.4	16 44.4	4.3	57.2
D 12	356 43.9	S 9 06.2	272 18.1	9.4	N16 48.7	4.2	57.2
A 13	11 44.0	05.3	286 46.5	9.4	16 52.9	4.1	57.1
Y 14	26 44.1	04.4	301 14.9	9.5	16 57.0	4.0	57.1
15	41 44.2 ..	03.5	315 43.4	9.4	17 01.0	3.9	57.1
16	56 44.3	02.5	330 11.8	9.5	17 04.9	3.8	57.0
17	71 44.4	01.6	344 40.3	9.5	17 08.7	3.7	57.0
18	86 44.5	S 9 00.7	359 08.8	9.6	N17 12.4	3.6	57.0
19	101 44.6	S 8 59.7	13 37.4	9.5	17 16.0	3.5	56.9
20	116 44.7	58.8	28 05.9	9.6	17 19.5	3.4	56.9
21	131 44.8 ..	57.9	42 34.5	9.6	17 22.9	3.3	56.9
22	146 44.9	56.9	57 03.1	9.6	17 26.2	3.2	56.8
23	161 45.0	56.0	71 31.7	9.6	17 29.4	3.1	56.8
26 00	176 45.1	S 8 55.1	86 00.3	9.7	N17 32.5	3.0	56.8
01	191 45.2	54.1	100 29.0	9.6	17 35.5	2.9	56.7
02	206 45.3	53.2	114 57.6	9.7	17 38.4	2.8	56.7
03	221 45.4 ..	52.3	129 26.3	9.7	17 41.2	2.7	56.7
04	236 45.5	51.4	143 55.0	9.8	17 43.9	2.6	56.6
05	251 45.6	50.4	158 23.8	9.7	17 46.5	2.5	56.6
T 06	266 45.7	S 8 49.5	172 52.5	9.8	N17 49.0	2.4	56.6
H 07	281 45.8	48.6	187 21.3	9.8	17 51.4	2.4	56.5
U 08	296 45.9	47.6	201 50.1	9.9	17 53.8	2.2	56.5
R 09	311 46.0 ..	46.7	216 19.0	9.8	17 56.0	2.1	56.5
S 10	326 46.1	45.7	230 47.8	9.9	17 58.1	2.0	56.4
D 11	341 46.2	44.8	245 16.7	9.9	18 00.1	1.9	56.4
A 12	356 46.3	S 8 43.9	259 45.6	9.9	N18 02.0	1.8	56.4
Y 13	11 46.4	42.9	274 14.5	10.0	18 03.8	1.8	56.3
14	26 46.5	42.0	288 43.5	10.0	18 05.6	1.6	56.3
15	41 46.6 ..	41.1	303 12.5	10.0	18 07.2	1.5	56.3
16	56 46.7	40.1	317 41.5	10.0	18 08.7	1.4	56.2
17	71 46.8	39.2	332 10.5	10.1	18 10.1	1.4	56.2
18	86 46.9	S 8 38.3	346 39.6	10.0	N18 11.5	1.2	56.2
19	101 47.0	37.3	1 08.6	10.1	18 12.7	1.1	56.1
20	116 47.1	36.4	15 37.7	10.2	18 13.8	1.1	56.1
21	131 47.2 ..	35.5	30 06.9	10.2	18 14.9	0.9	56.1
22	146 47.4	34.5	44 36.1	10.2	18 15.8	0.9	56.1
23	161 47.5	33.6	59 05.3	10.2	N18 16.7	0.7	56.0
	SD 16.2	d 0.9	SD 15.8		15.6		15.4

Lat.	Twilight Naut.	Twilight Civil	Sunrise	Moonrise 24	25	26	27
°	h m	h m	h m	h m	h m	h m	h m
N 72	05 31	06 49	08 00	07 30	07 23	07 11	▭
N 70	05 34	06 44	07 48	07 58	08 07	08 26	09 05
68	05 36	06 40	07 38	08 19	08 36	09 04	09 48
66	05 38	06 37	07 29	08 35	08 58	09 31	10 16
64	05 39	06 34	07 22	08 49	09 16	09 51	10 38
62	05 40	06 31	07 16	09 00	09 30	10 08	10 55
60	05 41	06 29	07 11	09 10	09 42	10 22	11 10
N 58	05 41	06 27	07 06	09 19	09 53	10 34	11 22
56	05 42	06 25	07 02	09 26	10 02	10 44	11 33
54	05 42	06 23	06 59	09 33	10 11	10 53	11 42
52	05 42	06 21	06 55	09 39	10 18	11 02	11 50
50	05 42	06 20	06 52	09 45	10 25	11 09	11 58
45	05 42	06 16	06 46	09 57	10 39	11 25	12 14
N 40	05 41	06 13	06 40	10 07	10 51	11 37	12 27
35	05 40	06 09	06 35	10 15	11 01	11 48	12 38
30	05 39	06 07	06 31	10 23	11 10	11 58	12 48
20	05 35	06 01	06 23	10 36	11 25	12 15	13 05
N 10	05 30	05 55	06 16	10 47	11 38	12 29	13 20
0	05 24	05 49	06 10	10 58	11 51	12 43	13 34
S 10	05 17	05 42	06 03	11 09	12 04	12 57	13 48
20	05 07	05 34	05 56	11 21	12 17	13 11	14 02
30	04 54	05 23	05 48	11 34	12 33	13 28	14 19
35	04 46	05 17	05 43	11 42	12 42	13 38	14 29
40	04 36	05 09	05 37	11 51	12 52	13 49	14 41
45	04 24	05 00	05 31	12 01	13 05	14 02	14 54
S 50	04 07	04 49	05 23	12 14	13 19	14 18	15 10
52	04 00	04 44	05 20	12 20	13 26	14 26	15 18
54	03 51	04 38	05 16	12 27	13 34	14 34	15 26
56	03 41	04 31	05 11	12 34	13 43	14 44	15 36
58	03 29	04 24	05 06	12 42	13 53	14 54	15 46
S 60	03 14	04 15	05 01	12 51	14 04	15 07	15 59

Lat.	Sunset	Twilight Civil	Twilight Naut.	Moonset 24	25	26	27
°	h m	h m	h m	h m	h m	h m	h m
N 72	16 28	17 39	18 58	01 45	03 42	05 44	▭
N 70	16 40	17 44	18 55	01 18	02 59	04 29	05 36
68	16 50	17 48	18 52	00 58	02 31	03 51	04 54
66	16 58	17 51	18 50	00 43	02 09	03 25	04 25
64	17 05	17 54	18 49	00 30	01 52	03 04	04 04
62	17 11	17 56	18 48	00 19	01 38	02 48	03 46
60	17 16	17 59	18 47	00 10	01 26	02 34	03 32
N 58	17 21	18 01	18 46	00 02	01 16	02 22	03 19
56	17 25	18 03	18 46	25 07	01 07	02 12	03 09
54	17 28	18 04	18 45	24 59	00 59	02 03	02 59
52	17 32	18 06	18 45	24 52	00 52	01 55	02 51
50	17 35	18 07	18 45	24 46	00 46	01 48	02 43
45	17 41	18 11	18 45	24 32	00 32	01 33	02 27
N 40	17 47	18 14	18 46	24 21	00 21	01 20	02 14
35	17 52	18 17	18 47	24 11	00 11	01 09	02 03
30	17 56	18 20	18 48	24 03	00 03	01 00	01 53
20	18 03	18 26	18 51	23 48	24 43	00 43	01 36
N 10	18 10	18 31	18 56	23 35	24 29	00 29	01 21
0	18 16	18 37	19 02	23 24	24 16	00 16	01 08
S 10	18 23	18 44	19 09	23 12	24 03	00 03	00 54
20	18 30	18 52	19 18	22 59	23 49	24 39	00 39
30	18 38	19 02	19 31	22 45	23 32	24 22	00 22
35	18 43	19 09	19 39	22 36	23 23	24 12	00 12
40	18 48	19 16	19 49	22 27	23 12	24 01	00 01
45	18 54	19 25	20 01	22 16	23 00	23 47	24 39
S 50	19 02	19 36	20 17	22 02	22 44	23 31	24 23
52	19 05	19 41	20 25	21 56	22 37	23 24	24 16
54	19 09	19 47	20 34	21 49	22 29	23 15	24 07
56	19 14	19 53	20 43	21 41	22 20	23 06	23 57
58	19 19	20 01	20 54	21 33	22 10	22 55	23 47
S 60	19 24	20 09	21 09	21 23	21 59	22 42	23 34

	SUN			MOON			
Day	Eqn. of Time 00ʰ	Eqn. of Time 12ʰ	Mer. Pass.	Mer. Pass. Upper	Mer. Pass. Lower	Age	Phase
d	m s	m s	h m	h m	h m	d	%
24	13 18	13 14	12 13	17 11	04 44	06	37
25	13 09	13 05	12 13	18 04	05 37	07	48
26	13 00	12 55	12 13	18 55	06 30	08	58

Let's do a few examples so you can better understand how to get exact GHA and declination for the time of observation.

On February 24, the observation of the sun is at 11:25:15 GMT—always GMT. The problem below shows how to find the GHA and declination GP for the time of the observation.

Feb 24

GHA 11:00 hrs   341°41.5   Dec S 9°29.4

Inc & Corr   + 6°18.8   d - 0.9   .4

GHA   Dec S 9° 29.0'

GHA   348 00.3

On May 20 observation of the sun is at 16:52:20 GMT. Find GHA and declination (GP) of the sun at the time of observation.

Nautical Almanac

16 hrs GHA   60°52.2   Dec N 20°00.2 d+.05

Inc & Corr   + 13°05.0   + .4

GHA   73° 57.2   Dec N 20°00.6

m 24	SUN PLANETS	ARIES	MOON	v or Corrⁿ d	v or Corrⁿ	v or Corrⁿ d	m 25	SUN PLANETS	ARIES	MOON	v or Corrⁿ d	v or Corrⁿ	v or Corrⁿ d
s	° ′	° ′	° ′	′ ′	′ ′	′ ′	s	° ′	° ′	° ′	′ ′	′ ′	′ ′
00	6 00·0	6 01·0	5 43·6	0·0 0·0	6·0 2·5	12·0 4·9	00	6 15·0	6 16·0	5 57·9	0·0 0·0	6·0 2·6	12·0 5·1
01	6 00·3	6 01·2	5 43·8	0·1 0·0	6·1 2·5	12·1 4·9	01	6 15·3	6 16·3	5 58·2	0·1 0·0	6·1 2·6	12·1 5·1
02	6 00·5	6 01·5	5 44·1	0·2 0·1	6·2 2·5	12·2 5·0	02	6 15·5	6 16·5	5 58·4	0·2 0·1	6·2 2·6	12·2 5·2
03	6 00·8	6 01·7	5 44·3	0·3 0·1	6·3 2·6	12·3 5·0	03	6 15·8	6 16·8	5 58·6	0·3 0·1	6·3 2·7	12·3 5·2
04	6 01·0	6 02·0	5 44·6	0·4 0·2	6·4 2·6	12·4 5·1	04	6 16·0	6 17·0	5 58·9	0·4 0·2	6·4 2·7	12·4 5·3
05	6 01·3	6 02·2	5 44·8	0·5 0·2	6·5 2·7	12·5 5·1	05	6 16·3	6 17·3	5 59·1	0·5 0·2	6·5 2·8	12·5 5·3
06	6 01·5	6 02·5	5 45·0	0·6 0·2	6·6 2·7	12·6 5·1	06	6 16·5	6 17·5	5 59·3	0·6 0·3	6·6 2·8	12·6 5·4
07	6 01·8	6 02·7	5 45·3	0·7 0·3	6·7 2·7	12·7 5·2	07	6 16·8	6 17·8	5 59·6	0·7 0·3	6·7 2·8	12·7 5·4
08	6 02·0	6 03·0	5 45·5	0·8 0·3	6·8 2·8	12·8 5·2	08	6 17·0	6 18·0	5 59·8	0·8 0·3	6·8 2·9	12·8 5·4
09	6 02·3	6 03·2	5 45·7	0·9 0·4	6·9 2·8	12·9 5·3	09	6 17·3	6 18·3	6 00·1	0·9 0·4	6·9 2·9	12·9 5·5
10	6 02·5	6 03·5	5 46·0	1·0 0·4	7·0 2·9	13·0 5·3	10	6 17·5	6 18·5	6 00·3	1·0 0·4	7·0 3·0	13·0 5·5
11	6 02·8	6 03·7	5 46·2	1·1 0·4	7·1 2·9	13·1 5·3	11	6 17·8	6 18·8	6 00·5	1·1 0·5	7·1 3·0	13·1 5·6
12	6 03·0	6 04·0	5 46·5	1·2 0·5	7·2 2·9	13·2 5·4	12	6 18·0	6 19·0	6 00·8	1·2 0·5	7·2 3·1	13·2 5·6
13	6 03·3	6 04·2	5 46·7	1·3 0·5	7·3 3·0	13·3 5·4	13	6 18·3	6 19·3	6 01·0	1·3 0·6	7·3 3·1	13·3 5·7
14	6 03·5	6 04·5	5 46·9	1·4 0·6	7·4 3·0	13·4 5·5	14	6 18·5	6 19·5	6 01·3	1·4 0·6	7·4 3·1	13·4 5·7
15	6 03·8	6 04·7	5 47·2	1·5 0·6	7·5 3·1	13·5 5·5	15	6 18·8	6 19·8	6 01·5	1·5 0·6	7·5 3·2	13·5 5·7
16	6 04·0	6 05·0	5 47·4	1·6 0·7	7·6 3·1	13·6 5·6	16	6 19·0	6 20·0	6 01·7	1·6 0·7	7·6 3·2	13·6 5·8
17	6 04·3	6 05·2	5 47·7	1·7 0·7	7·7 3·1	13·7 5·6	17	6 19·3	6 20·3	6 02·0	1·7 0·7	7·7 3·3	13·7 5·8
18	6 04·5	6 05·5	5 47·9	1·8 0·7	7·8 3·2	13·8 5·6	18	6 19·5	6 20·5	6 02·2	1·8 0·8	7·8 3·3	13·8 5·9
19	6 04·8	6 05·7	5 48·1	1·9 0·8	7·9 3·2	13·9 5·7	19	6 19·8	6 20·8	6 02·5	1·9 0·8	7·9 3·4	13·9 5·9
20	6 05·0	6 06·0	5 48·4	2·0 0·8	8·0 3·3	14·0 5·7	20	6 20·0	6 21·0	6 02·7	2·0 0·9	8·0 3·4	14·0 6·0
21	6 05·3	6 06·3	5 48·6	2·1 0·9	8·1 3·3	14·1 5·8	21	6 20·3	6 21·3	6 02·9	2·1 0·9	8·1 3·4	14·1 6·0
22	6 05·5	6 06·5	5 48·8	2·2 0·9	8·2 3·3	14·2 5·8	22	6 20·5	6 21·5	6 03·2	2·2 0·9	8·2 3·5	14·2 6·0
23	6 05·8	6 06·8	5 49·1	2·3 0·9	8·3 3·4	14·3 5·8	23	6 20·8	6 21·8	6 03·4	2·3 1·0	8·3 3·5	14·3 6·1
24	6 06·0	6 07·0	5 49·3	2·4 1·0	8·4 3·4	14·4 5·9	24	6 21·0	6 22·0	6 03·6	2·4 1·0	8·4 3·6	14·4 6·1

2015 MAY 19, 20, 21 (TUES., WED., THURS.)   103

SUN and MOON

UT (d h)	SUN GHA	SUN Dec	MOON GHA	v	MOON Dec	d	HP
19 00	180 53.5	N19 38.9	168 53.1	7.4	N17 20.7	3.7	58.4
01	195 53.5	39.4	183 19.5	7.4	17 24.4	3.6	58.4
02	210 53.5	40.0	197 45.9	7.4	17 28.0	3.4	58.4
03	225 53.5 ..	40.5	212 12.3	7.4	17 31.4	3.4	58.4
04	240 53.4	41.1	226 38.7	7.4	17 34.8	3.2	58.3
05	255 53.4	41.6	241 05.1	7.5	17 38.0	3.2	58.3
T 06	270 53.4	N19 42.2	255 31.6	7.5	N17 41.2	3.0	58.3
U 07	285 53.3	42.7	269 58.1	7.4	17 44.2	2.9	58.2
E 08	300 53.3	43.2	284 24.5	7.5	17 47.1	2.8	58.2
S 09	315 53.3 ..	43.8	298 51.0	7.6	17 49.9	2.6	58.2
D 10	330 53.3	44.3	313 17.6	7.5	17 52.5	2.6	58.1
A 11	345 53.2	44.8	327 44.1	7.6	17 55.1	2.4	58.1
Y 12	0 53.2	N19 45.4	342 10.7	7.6	N17 57.5	2.4	58.1
13	15 53.2	45.9	356 37.3	7.6	17 59.9	2.2	58.1
14	30 53.1	46.5	11 03.9	7.6	18 02.1	2.1	58.0
15	45 53.1 ..	47.0	25 30.5	7.7	18 04.2	2.0	58.0
16	60 53.1	47.5	39 57.2	7.7	18 06.2	1.9	58.0
17	75 53.0	48.1	54 23.9	7.7	18 08.1	1.8	57.9
18	90 53.0	N19 48.6	68 50.6	7.7	N18 09.9	1.7	57.9
19	105 53.0	49.1	83 17.3	7.8	18 11.6	1.5	57.9
20	120 52.9	49.7	97 44.1	7.8	18 13.1	1.5	57.8
21	135 52.9 ..	50.2	112 10.9	7.9	18 14.6	1.3	57.8
22	150 52.9	50.7	126 37.8	7.8	18 15.9	1.2	57.8
23	165 52.8	51.2	141 04.6	7.9	18 17.1	1.1	57.7
20 00	180 52.8	N19 51.8	155 31.5	8.0	N18 18.2	1.0	57.7
01	195 52.8	52.3	169 58.5	7.9	18 19.2	0.9	57.7
02	210 52.7	52.8	184 25.4	8.0	18 20.1	0.8	57.7
03	225 52.7 ..	53.4	198 52.4	8.1	18 20.9	0.7	57.6
04	240 52.7	53.9	213 19.5	8.1	18 21.6	0.5	57.6
05	255 52.6	54.4	227 46.6	8.1	18 22.1	0.5	57.6
W 06	270 52.6	N19 54.9	242 13.7	8.1	N18 22.6	0.3	57.5
E 07	285 52.6	55.5	256 40.8	8.2	18 22.9	0.3	57.5
D 08	300 52.5	56.0	271 08.0	8.3	18 23.2	0.1	57.5
N 09	315 52.5 ..	56.5	285 35.3	8.2	18 23.3	0.0	57.4
E 10	330 52.5	57.0	300 02.5	8.3	18 23.3	0.1	57.4
S 11	345 52.4	57.6	314 29.8	8.4	18 23.2	0.1	57.4
D 12	0 52.4	N19 58.1	328 57.2	8.4	N18 23.1	0.4	57.3
A 13	15 52.4	58.6	343 24.6	8.5	18 22.7	0.4	57.3
Y 14	30 52.3	59.1	357 52.1	8.4	18 22.3	0.5	57.3
15	45 52.3	19 59.6	12 19.5	8.6	18 21.8	0.6	57.2
16	60 52.2	20 00.2	26 47.1	8.6	18 21.2	0.7	57.2
17	75 52.2	00.7	41 14.7	8.6	18 20.5	0.8	57.2
18	90 52.2	N20 01.2	55 42.3	8.7	N18 19.7	1.0	57.1
19	105 52.1	01.7	70 10.0	8.7	18 18.7	1.0	57.1
20	120 52.1	02.2	84 37.7	8.8	18 17.7	1.1	57.1
21	135 52.1 ..	02.8	99 05.5	8.8	18 16.6	1.3	57.0
22	150 52.0	03.3	113 33.3	8.9	18 15.3	1.3	57.0
23	165 52.0	03.8	128 01.2	8.9	18 14.0	1.5	57.0
21 00	180 51.9	N20 04.3	142 29.1	9.0	N18 12.5	1.5	56.9
01	195 51.9	04.8	156 57.1	9.0	18 11.0	1.6	56.9
02	210 51.9	05.3	171 25.1	9.1	18 09.4	1.8	56.9
03	225 51.8 ..	05.8	185 53.2	9.1	18 07.6	1.8	56.9
04	240 51.8	06.4	200 21.3	9.2	18 05.8	2.0	56.8
05	255 51.7	06.9	214 49.5	9.2	18 03.8	2.0	56.8
T 06	270 51.7	N20 07.4	229 17.7	9.3	N18 01.8	2.1	56.8
H 07	285 51.7	07.9	243 46.0	9.4	17 59.7	2.3	56.7
U 08	300 51.6	08.4	258 14.4	9.4	17 57.4	2.3	56.7
R 09	315 51.6 ..	08.9	272 42.8	9.4	17 55.1	2.4	56.7
S 10	330 51.5	09.4	287 11.2	9.5	17 52.7	2.6	56.6
D 11	345 51.5	09.9	301 39.7	9.6	17 50.1	2.6	56.6
A 12	0 51.5	N20 10.4	316 08.3	9.6	N17 47.5	2.7	56.6
Y 13	15 51.4	10.9	330 36.9	9.7	17 44.8	2.8	56.5
14	30 51.4	11.5	345 05.6	9.8	17 42.0	2.9	56.5
15	45 51.3 ..	12.0	359 34.4	9.8	17 39.1	3.0	56.5
16	60 51.3	12.5	14 03.2	9.8	17 36.1	3.0	56.4
17	75 51.2	13.0	28 32.0	9.9	17 33.1	3.2	56.4
18	90 51.2	N20 13.5	43 00.9	10.0	N17 29.9	3.3	56.4
19	105 51.2	14.0	57 29.9	10.1	17 26.6	3.3	56.4
20	120 51.1	14.5	71 59.0	10.0	17 23.3	3.4	56.3
21	135 51.1 ..	15.0	86 28.0	10.2	17 19.9	3.5	56.3
22	150 51.0	15.5	100 57.2	10.2	17 16.4	3.7	56.3
23	165 51.0	16.0	115 26.4	10.3	N17 12.7	3.7	56.2
	SD 15.8	d 0.5	SD 15.8		15.6		15.4

Twilight / Sunrise / Moonrise

Lat.	Naut.	Civil	Sunrise	Moonrise 19	20	21	22
N 72	□	□	□	01 54	□	□	05 01
N 70	□	□	□	02 54	03 27	04 28	05 51
68	////	////	01 19	03 29	04 09	05 08	06 23
66	////	////	02 04	03 54	04 37	05 36	06 46
64	////	00 21	02 33	04 14	04 59	05 57	07 04
62	////	01 31	02 54	04 30	05 16	06 14	07 19
60	////	02 04	03 12	04 43	05 31	06 28	07 32
N 58	00 18	02 28	03 27	04 54	05 43	06 40	07 43
56	01 22	02 47	03 39	05 05	05 54	06 50	07 52
54	01 53	03 03	03 50	05 13	06 03	07 00	08 00
52	02 15	03 16	04 00	05 21	06 12	07 08	08 08
50	02 33	03 28	04 08	05 29	06 19	07 15	08 15
45	03 07	03 51	04 26	05 44	06 36	07 31	08 29
N 40	03 31	04 10	04 41	05 57	06 49	07 44	08 41
35	03 50	04 25	04 53	06 07	07 00	07 55	08 51
30	04 06	04 38	05 04	06 17	07 10	08 05	09 00
20	04 30	04 59	05 22	06 33	07 27	08 21	09 15
N 10	04 49	05 16	05 38	06 47	07 42	08 36	09 28
0	05 05	05 31	05 53	07 01	07 56	08 49	09 40
S 10	05 20	05 45	06 08	07 14	08 10	09 03	09 53
20	05 33	06 00	06 23	07 29	08 25	09 17	10 06
30	05 46	06 15	06 41	07 45	08 42	09 34	10 21
35	05 53	06 24	06 51	07 55	08 52	09 44	10 30
40	06 00	06 33	07 02	08 06	09 03	09 55	10 40
45	06 08	06 44	07 16	08 19	09 17	10 08	10 51
S 50	06 17	06 57	07 33	08 35	09 33	10 23	11 05
52	06 21	07 02	07 41	08 42	09 41	10 31	11 12
54	06 25	07 09	07 49	08 50	09 49	10 39	11 19
56	06 29	07 16	07 59	09 00	09 59	10 48	11 27
58	06 34	07 23	08 10	09 10	10 10	10 58	11 37
S 60	06 39	07 32	08 23	09 22	10 23	11 10	11 47

Sunset / Twilight / Moonset

Lat.	Sunset	Twilight Civil	Naut.	Moonset 19	20	21	22
N 72	□	□	□	23 55	24 46	00 46	01 10
N 70	□	////	////	23 13	24 06	00 06	00 38
68	22 40	////	////	22 45	23 38	24 14	00 14
66	21 53	////	////	22 23	23 17	23 56	24 24
64	21 23	////	////	22 06	23 01	23 40	24 11
62	21 00	22 26	////	21 51	22 45	23 28	24 00
60	20 43	21 51	////	21 39	22 33	23 17	23 51
N 58	20 28	21 27	////	21 28	22 23	23 07	23 43
56	20 15	21 07	22 35	21 19	22 13	22 58	23 35
54	20 04	20 52	22 03	21 10	22 05	22 51	23 29
52	19 54	20 38	21 40	21 03	21 57	22 44	23 23
50	19 46	20 26	21 21	20 47	21 41	22 29	23 10
45	19 27	20 02	20 47	20 47	21 41	22 29	23 10
N 40	19 13	19 44	20 23	20 34	21 28	22 17	22 59
35	19 00	19 29	20 03	20 23	21 17	22 06	22 50
30	18 49	19 16	19 48	20 13	21 07	21 57	22 42
20	18 31	18 55	19 23	19 56	20 50	21 41	22 28
N 10	18 15	18 37	19 04	19 41	20 36	21 27	22 16
0	18 00	18 22	18 48	19 27	20 22	21 14	22 04
S 10	17 45	18 08	18 33	19 13	20 08	21 01	21 52
20	17 30	17 53	18 20	18 59	19 53	20 47	21 40
30	17 12	17 38	18 07	18 42	19 36	20 31	21 26
35	17 02	17 29	18 00	18 32	19 26	20 22	21 18
40	16 50	17 20	17 53	18 21	19 15	20 11	21 08
45	16 36	17 09	17 45	18 07	19 01	19 58	20 57
S 50	16 20	16 56	17 36	17 51	18 45	19 43	20 43
52	16 12	16 50	17 32	17 44	18 37	19 36	20 37
54	16 03	16 44	17 28	17 35	18 29	19 28	20 30
56	15 53	16 37	17 23	17 26	18 19	19 19	20 22
58	15 42	16 29	17 18	17 15	18 09	19 09	20 14
S 60	15 29	16 20	17 13	17 03	17 56	18 57	20 04

SUN and MOON

Day	SUN Eqn. of Time 00h	12h	Mer. Pass.	MOON Mer. Pass. Upper	Lower	Age	Phase
19	03 34	03 33	11 56	13 14	00 46	01	2
20	03 31	03 30	11 57	14 09	01 42	02	7
21	03 28	03 26	11 57	15 02	02 36	03	13

52ᵐ INCREMENTS AND CORRECTIONS 53ᵐ

52	SUN PLANETS	ARIES	MOON	v or Corrn d	v or Corrn d	v or Corrn d	53	SUN PLANETS	ARIES	MOON	v or Corrn d	v or Corrn d	v or Corrn d
00	13 00·0	13 02·1	12 24·5	0·0 0·0	6·0 5·3	12·0 10·5	00	13 15·0	13 17·2	12 38·8	0·0 0·0	6·0 5·4	12·0 10·7
01	13 00·3	13 02·4	12 24·7	0·1 0·1	6·1 5·3	12·1 10·6	01	13 15·3	13 17·4	12 39·0	0·1 0·1	6·1 5·4	12·1 10·8
02	13 00·5	13 02·6	12 25·2	0·2 0·2	6·2 5·4	12·2 10·7	02	13 15·5	13 17·7	12 39·3	0·2 0·2	6·2 5·5	12·2 10·9
03	13 00·8	13 02·9	12 25·2	0·3 0·3	6·3 5·5	12·3 10·8	03	13 15·8	13 17·9	12 39·5	0·3 0·3	6·3 5·6	12·3 11·0
04	13 01·0	13 03·1	12 25·4	0·4 0·4	6·4 5·6	12·4 10·9	04	13 16·0	13 18·2	12 39·7	0·4 0·4	6·4 5·7	12·4 11·1
05	13 01·3	13 03·4	12 25·7	0·5 0·4	6·5 5·7	12·5 10·9	05	13 16·3	13 18·4	12 40·0	0·5 0·4	6·5 5·8	12·5 11·1
06	13 01·5	13 03·6	12 25·9	0·6 0·5	6·6 5·8	12·6 11·0	06	13 16·5	13 18·7	12 40·2	0·6 0·5	6·6 5·9	12·6 11·2
07	13 01·8	13 03·9	12 26·1	0·7 0·6	6·7 5·9	12·7 11·1	07	13 16·8	13 18·9	12 40·5	0·7 0·6	6·7 6·0	12·7 11·3
08	13 02·0	13 04·1	12 26·4	0·8 0·7	6·8 6·0	12·8 11·2	08	13 17·0	13 19·2	12 40·7	0·8 0·7	6·8 6·1	12·8 11·4
09	13 02·3	13 04·4	12 26·6	0·9 0·8	6·9 6·0	12·9 11·3	09	13 17·3	13 19·4	12 40·9	0·9 0·8	6·9 6·2	12·9 11·5
10	13 02·5	13 04·6	12 26·9	1·0 0·9	7·0 6·1	13·0 11·4	10	13 17·5	13 19·7	12 41·2	1·0 0·9	7·0 6·2	13·0 11·6
11	13 02·8	13 04·9	12 27·1	1·1 1·0	7·1 6·2	13·1 11·5	11	13 17·8	13 19·9	12 41·4	1·1 1·0	7·1 6·3	13·1 11·7
12	13 03·0	13 05·1	12 27·3	1·2 1·1	7·2 6·3	13·2 11·6	12	13 18·0	13 20·2	12 41·6	1·2 1·1	7·2 6·4	13·2 11·8
13	13 03·3	13 05·4	12 27·6	1·3 1·1	7·3 6·4	13·3 11·6	13	13 18·3	13 20·4	12 41·9	1·3 1·2	7·3 6·5	13·3 11·9
14	13 03·5	13 05·6	12 27·8	1·4 1·2	7·4 6·5	13·4 11·7	14	13 18·5	13 20·7	12 42·1	1·4 1·2	7·4 6·6	13·4 11·9
15	13 03·8	13 05·9	12 28·0	1·5 1·3	7·5 6·6	13·5 11·8	15	13 18·8	13 20·9	12 42·4	1·5 1·3	7·5 6·7	13·5 12·0
16	13 04·0	13 06·1	12 28·3	1·6 1·4	7·6 6·7	13·6 11·9	16	13 19·0	13 21·2	12 42·6	1·6 1·4	7·6 6·8	13·6 12·1
17	13 04·3	13 06·4	12 28·5	1·7 1·5	7·7 6·7	13·7 12·0	17	13 19·3	13 21·4	12 42·8	1·7 1·5	7·7 6·9	13·7 12·2
18	13 04·5	13 06·6	12 28·8	1·8 1·6	7·8 6·8	13·8 12·1	18	13 19·5	13 21·7	12 43·1	1·8 1·6	7·8 7·0	13·8 12·3
19	13 04·8	13 06·9	12 29·0	1·9 1·7	7·9 6·9	13·9 12·2	19	13 19·8	13 21·9	12 43·3	1·9 1·7	7·9 7·0	13·9 12·4
20	13 05·0	13 07·1	12 29·2	2·0 1·8	8·0 7·0	14·0 12·3	20	13 20·0	13 22·2	12 43·6	2·0 1·8	8·0 7·1	14·0 12·5
21	13 05·3	13 07·4	12 29·5	2·1 1·8	8·1 7·1	14·1 12·3	21	13 20·3	13 22·4	12 43·8	2·1 1·9	8·1 7·2	14·1 12·6
22	13 05·5	13 07·7	12 29·7	2·2 1·9	8·2 7·2	14·2 12·4	22	13 20·5	13 22·7	12 44·0	2·2 2·0	8·2 7·3	14·2 12·7
23	13 05·8	13 07·9	12 30·0	2·3 2·0	8·3 7·3	14·3 12·5	23	13 20·8	13 22·9	12 44·3	2·3 2·1	8·3 7·4	14·3 12·8
24	13 06·0	13 08·2	12 30·2	2·4 2·1	8·4 7·4	14·4 12·6	24	13 21·0	13 23·2	12 44·5	2·4 2·1	8·4 7·5	14·4 12·8
25	13 06·3	13 08·4	12 30·4	2·5 2·2	8·5 7·4	14·5 12·7	25	13 21·3	13 23·4	12 44·7	2·5 2·2	8·5 7·6	14·5 12·9
26	13 06·5	13 08·7	12 30·7	2·6 2·3	8·6 7·5	14·6 12·8	26	13 21·5	13 23·7	12 45·0	2·6 2·3	8·6 7·7	14·6 13·0
27	13 06·8	13 08·9	12 31·1	2·7 2·4	8·7 7·6	14·7 12·9	27	13 21·8	13 23·9	12 45·2	2·7 2·4	8·7 7·8	14·7 13·1
28	13 07·0	13 09·2	12 31·1	2·8 2·5	8·8 7·7	14·8 13·0	28	13 22·0	13 24·2	12 45·5	2·8 2·5	8·8 7·8	14·8 13·2
29	13 07·3	13 09·4	12 31·4	2·9 2·5	8·9 7·8	14·9 13·0	29	13 22·3	13 24·4	12 45·7	2·9 2·6	8·9 7·9	14·9 13·3
30	13 07·5	13 09·7	12 31·6	3·0 2·6	9·0 7·9	15·0 13·1	30	13 22·5	13 24·7	12 45·9	3·0 2·7	9·0 8·0	15·0 13·4
31	13 07·8	13 09·9	12 31·9	3·1 2·7	9·1 8·0	15·1 13·2	31	13 22·8	13 24·9	12 46·2	3·1 2·8	9·1 8·1	15·1 13·5
32	13 08·0	13 10·2	12 32·1	3·2 2·8	9·2 8·0	15·2 13·3	32	13 23·0	13 25·2	12 46·4	3·2 2·9	9·2 8·2	15·2 13·6
33	13 08·3	13 10·4	12 32·3	3·3 2·9	9·3 8·1	15·3 13·4	33	13 23·3	13 25·4	12 46·7	3·3 2·9	9·3 8·3	15·3 13·6
34	13 08·5	13 10·7	12 32·6	3·4 3·0	9·4 8·2	15·4 13·5	34	13 23·5	13 25·7	12 46·9	3·4 3·0	9·4 8·4	15·4 13·7
35	13 08·8	13 10·9	12 32·8	3·5 3·1	9·5 8·3	15·5 13·6	35	13 23·8	13 26·0	12 47·1	3·5 3·1	9·5 8·5	15·5 13·8
36	13 09·0	13 11·2	12 33·1	3·6 3·2	9·6 8·4	15·6 13·7	36	13 24·0	13 26·2	12 47·4	3·6 3·2	9·6 8·6	15·6 13·9
37	13 09·3	13 11·4	12 33·3	3·7 3·2	9·7 8·5	15·7 13·7	37	13 24·3	13 26·5	12 47·6	3·7 3·3	9·7 8·6	15·7 14·0
38	13 09·5	13 11·7	12 33·5	3·8 3·3	9·8 8·6	15·8 13·8	38	13 24·5	13 26·7	12 47·9	3·8 3·4	9·8 8·7	15·8 14·1
39	13 09·8	13 11·9	12 33·8	3·9 3·4	9·9 8·7	15·9 13·9	39	13 24·8	13 27·0	12 48·1	3·9 3·5	9·9 8·8	15·9 14·2
40	13 10·0	13 12·2	12 34·0	4·0 3·5	10·0 8·8	16·0 14·0	40	13 25·0	13 27·2	12 48·3	4·0 3·6	10·0 8·9	16·0 14·3
41	13 10·3	13 12·4	12 34·2	4·1 3·6	10·1 8·8	16·1 14·1	41	13 25·3	13 27·5	12 48·6	4·1 3·7	10·1 9·0	16·1 14·4
42	13 10·5	13 12·7	12 34·5	4·2 3·7	10·2 8·9	16·2 14·2	42	13 25·5	13 27·7	12 48·8	4·2 3·7	10·2 9·1	16·2 14·4
43	13 10·8	13 12·9	12 34·7	4·3 3·8	10·3 9·0	16·3 14·3	43	13 25·8	13 28·0	12 49·0	4·3 3·8	10·3 9·2	16·3 14·5
44	13 11·0	13 13·2	12 35·0	4·4 3·9	10·4 9·1	16·4 14·4	44	13 26·0	13 28·2	12 49·3	4·4 3·9	10·4 9·3	16·4 14·6
45	13 11·3	13 13·4	12 35·2	4·5 3·9	10·5 9·2	16·5 14·4	45	13 26·3	13 28·5	12 49·5	4·5 4·0	10·5 9·4	16·5 14·7
46	13 11·5	13 13·7	12 35·4	4·6 4·0	10·6 9·3	16·6 14·5	46	13 26·5	13 28·7	12 49·8	4·6 4·1	10·6 9·5	16·6 14·8
47	13 11·8	13 13·9	12 35·7	4·7 4·1	10·7 9·4	16·7 14·6	47	13 26·8	13 29·0	12 50·0	4·7 4·2	10·7 9·5	16·7 14·9
48	13 12·0	13 14·2	12 35·9	4·8 4·2	10·8 9·5	16·8 14·7	48	13 27·0	13 29·2	12 50·2	4·8 4·3	10·8 9·6	16·8 15·0
49	13 12·3	13 14·4	12 36·2	4·9 4·3	10·9 9·5	16·9 14·8	49	13 27·3	13 29·5	12 50·5	4·9 4·4	10·9 9·7	16·9 15·1
50	13 12·5	13 14·7	12 36·4	5·0 4·4	11·0 9·6	17·0 14·9	50	13 27·5	13 29·7	12 50·7	5·0 4·5	11·0 9·8	17·0 15·2
51	13 12·8	13 14·9	12 36·6	5·1 4·5	11·1 9·7	17·1 15·0	51	13 27·8	13 30·0	12 51·0	5·1 4·5	11·1 9·9	17·1 15·2
52	13 13·0	13 15·2	12 36·9	5·2 4·6	11·2 9·8	17·2 15·1	52	13 28·0	13 30·2	12 51·2	5·2 4·6	11·2 10·0	17·2 15·3
53	13 13·3	13 15·4	12 37·1	5·3 4·6	11·3 9·9	17·3 15·1	53	13 28·3	13 30·5	12 51·4	5·3 4·7	11·3 10·1	17·3 15·4
54	13 13·5	13 15·7	12 37·4	5·4 4·7	11·4 10·0	17·4 15·2	54	13 28·5	13 30·7	12 51·7	5·4 4·8	11·4 10·2	17·4 15·5
55	13 13·8	13 15·9	12 37·6	5·5 4·8	11·5 10·1	17·5 15·3	55	13 28·8	13 31·0	12 51·9	5·5 4·9	11·5 10·3	17·5 15·6
56	13 14·0	13 16·2	12 37·8	5·6 4·9	11·6 10·2	17·6 15·4	56	13 29·0	13 31·2	12 52·1	5·6 5·0	11·6 10·3	17·6 15·7
57	13 14·3	13 16·4	12 38·1	5·7 5·0	11·7 10·2	17·7 15·5	57	13 29·3	13 31·5	12 52·4	5·7 5·1	11·7 10·4	17·7 15·8
58	13 14·5	13 16·7	12 38·3	5·8 5·1	11·8 10·3	17·8 15·6	58	13 29·5	13 31·7	12 52·6	5·8 5·2	11·8 10·5	17·8 15·9
59	13 14·8	13 16·9	12 38·5	5·9 5·2	11·9 10·4	17·9 15·7	59	13 29·8	13 32·0	12 52·9	5·9 5·3	11·9 10·6	17·9 16·0
60	13 15·0	13 17·2	12 38·8	6·0 5·3	12·0 10·5	18·0 15·8	60	13 30·0	13 32·2	12 53·1	6·0 5·4	12·0 10·7	18·0 16·1

Basic math reminders

Before we move forward, we need to establish some ground rules about the way to add and subtract numbers in celestial navigation. It is a bit confusing since we are using minutes as both arc and time. (If you find this frustrating, blame it on the Babylonians who decided that a degree of arc should be broken up into minutes and that time also would have minutes.) Don't be hoodwinked, though. Time is time, even in navigation. Sixty minutes to an hour, sixty seconds to a minute. Arc is written in degrees, minutes, and tenths of minutes. When adding and subtracting, we must always remember the difference. When discussing arc, we refer to degrees, minutes, and tenths of minutes, not degrees, minutes, and seconds.

Ninety percent of the errors that occur in celestial navigation have to do less with the skills of taking a sight and more to do with math errors, which are often quite rudimentary. So when doing math, give at least some attention to the task at hand, unless you are one of those lucky souls, like a natural-born speller, who just gets numbers.

For the sake of clarity, indulge me while I review the basics. And I speak here not as an instructor but as a fellow traveler. When adding time, we use hours, minutes, and seconds. So let's say the time in GMT is 12:15:48. To this we are adding 48 minutes and 35 seconds. The resulting answer is 12 hours, 63 minutes, and 83 seconds. Now we know that in this form there is no such time. There is no 63 minutes nor is there an 83 seconds, so we need to convert seconds to minutes and minutes to hours; thus, 12:63:83 becomes 13:04:23.

11:98:78
11:98:78

Another example is 6:52:51 + 5:46:27 = 11:99:18, which in the real world is 12:39:18.

Another: 2:21:13 + 1:15:30 + 3:36:43.

Now let's subtract: 8:15:30 - 5:07:28. This is easy. It equals 3:08:02.

Now try this 10:22:25 - 8:35:42 = 1:46:43. Okay?

So in doing these equations, you'll constantly be converting sixty seconds to one minute and sixty minutes to one hour.

Now let's take a look at arc, which is based on a base 10 system. Sixty minutes equals 1° and 10/10 of a minute equals 1 minute of arc. Confusing? You betcha, but you'll get used to it.

Time for more practice: Let's try 5°25.8' + 6°40.4' = 11°66.2', which in our world is actually 12°06.2'.

Let's try another: 48°35.6' + 17°45.9' = 65°81.5', which is, in reality, 66°21.5'. Get it?

Or subtract 17°45.9' - 8°52.1'. In this example I convert 17°45.9' to 16°105.9', then I subtract the 8°52.1' and I come up with the answer of 8°53.8'.

So remember, always, degrees, minutes, tenths of minutes for arc, based on base 10, and hours, minutes, and seconds for time, based on base 60.

There is one last thing to consider before we move on. When working with arc, there will be times when you will be subtracting a larger number from a smaller one. Local Hour Angle, which we will discuss, can never be a negative number, so there will be times when we have to add 360° (a whole circle) to a smaller number. For example, 75°35.8' - 95°27.2' can't be done you say. Well, add 360° to 75° and get

435°. Then subtract the 95°27.2' - 435°35.8' and you get an answer of 340°8.6'. So add 360° to the smaller number if you are subtracting a larger number from it.

Local Hour Angle

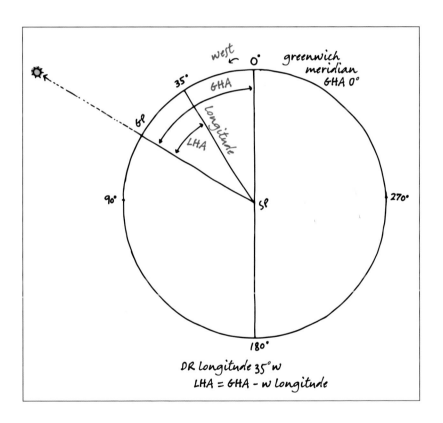

west 0°
greenwich
meridian
GHA 0°
35°
GHA
GP
longitude
LHA
90°
270°
SP
180°

DR longitude 35° W
LHA = GHA − W longitude

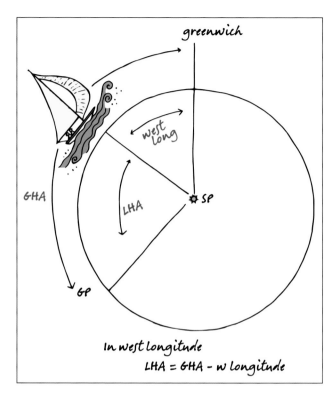

greenwich

west long

GHA

LHA

☀ SP

GP

In west longitude
LHA = GHA - w longitude

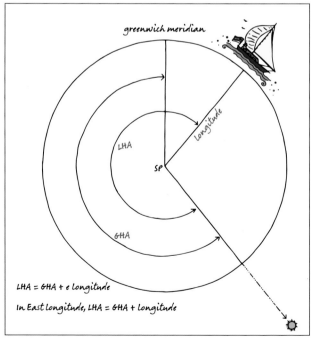

greenwich meridian

longitude

LHA

SP

GHA

LHA = GHA + e longitude

In East longitude, LHA = GHA + longitude

So now we understand GHA and how to find it. Is that all there is to it? Well, it could be if we were always at the Greenwich meridian, but usually we are somewhere else, sailing on the wine-dark seas on our way from one exciting place to another. So then, how do we measure the Greenwich Hour Angle from where we are? We already have stated that the GHA is measured in a westerly direction commencing at the Greenwich meridian. So how do we measure the angular distance from our location to the GP of the sun?

I now introduce a new term called Local Hour Angle (LHA), which is the westerly difference in arc from our location or DR position to the GP of the sun. It is easy to understand by looking at the diagrams on the previous page. Also, there is a simple formula that will keep you always on the right track: In westerly longitude, LHA equals GHA minus west longitude. After studying the accompanying diagram, this should appear clear. If, on the other hand, we are sailing in easterly longitudes, then the LHA equals GHA plus east longitude. Remember, it is important first to find the GHA of the GP of the sun using the *Nautical Almanac* for the time of the observation, and then to extract from that the LHA, which is predicated on the DR longitude. LHA is very important because we need an LHA in order to enter into the sight reduction tables. If you are using a computer program or a calculator, the LHA is moot; those tools can calculate it for you. But for the sake of understanding as much of the process as possible, we will deal with the LHA as an integral part of our learning. Again, GHA is measured from the Greenwich Hour Angle 0°, or Greenwich meridian in a westerly direction to the GP of the sun. LHA, or the observer's angular distance to the GP, is calculated by subtracting longitude from GHA in western longitude, or adding the longitude to the GHA in eastern longitude. Diagrams are good to make, so get into the habit of drawing the GHA and LHA so that it becomes second nature.

A note here about making diagrams. I personally find making simple diagrams very helpful when doing celestial navigation. For some, the numbers explain all, but others like me need graphics to help see what I am doing. It is not a bad habit to get into. When I make a simple GHA or LHA diagram I just draw a circle and label Greenwich. In the center of the circle I label it SP, meaning South Pole. (I presume that I am in space looking up at the South Pole.) I do this because that view allows me to have west to my left, which is what I am used to seeing on maps. It's just easier for me. But you can either look down on the North Pole, or up at the South Pole as long as you are consistent.

Let's do an example that demonstrates what we are talking about.

On May 10 (see page 17), we are at a DR of N 35°25' by W 68°19'. At 1100 hours GMT, according to the *Nautical Almanac*, the GHA of the sun is 345°54.0. In order to find the LHA we subtract the DR longitude from the GHA:

GHA at 1100 hours	345°54.0
DR long	− 68°19'
=	
LHA of observer	277°35'

What this means is that the angular distance of the GP of the sun is 277°35' west of the observer, and because we know that in celestial navigation that we are the center of the universe, we always need to measure the GP of the sun from our exact location. Remember this concept in the discussion on Assumed Position.

First, let's review what we have learned so far. We know that the core of celestial navigation is solving for our distance and bearing (azimuth) in relation to the Geographical Position (GP) of the sun. We find the exact GP of the sun by using the *Nautical Almanac*, which lists the declination and GHA of the sun for every hour, minute, and second of a specific day. We have also found that by using Increments and Corrections tables in the *Nautical Almanac* we find the exact declination and GHA of the sun at whatever time we took our observation.

We also know that the *Nautical Almanac* operates with time set on Greenwich. Celestial navigation always uses Greenwich Time. We also have learned that we need to find the LHA, which is our distance in arc to the GP, unless of course we are at the Greenwich meridian, in which case our LHA would equal the Greenwich Hour Angle (GHA). We calculate our LHA by using the formula LHA = GHA - W Longitude or LHA = GHA + E Longitude. Practice these until you are accustomed to the procedure.

Another thing to remember is that the d correction for the change in declination is at the bottom of the daily pages in the *Nautical Almanac*. This number represents the hourly change in the declination. It can be either added to or subtracted from the declination based on examination of the tables. The d correction is an arrow that points to the final correction that is found in the Increments and Corrections table. The *Almanac* is laid out in a very cumbersome fashion that takes a bit of getting used to. Ruminate on these concepts. They are key.

Assumed Position

The concept of Assumed Position is the first one of two the important building blocks in modern celestial navigation. Another is the Sumner Line of Position. Some brief background: In 1837, American Captain Thomas Sumner, approaching the English coast, discovered that by taking a series of sights and using different latitudes that the position of the celestial object was at right angles to his bearing line. Captain Sumner also came up with the concept of circles of equal altitude (we saw this at the beginning when we walked around the flagpole), and that a line or segment of that Circle of Position is actually a LOP whose bearing is at right angles to the celestial object. Remember that a circle is just a polygon with an infinite number of lines. The very small segment of the Circle of Position that we are concerned with when we take an observation is so small relative to the great size of the circle that is a segment of that circle, a straight line.

The next development essential to understanding modern celestial navigation was conceived by Marcq St. Hilaire, a Frenchman who perfected what Captain Sumner first posited. In the 1870s, St. Hilaire developed what he called the *methode du pointe rapproche*, or the method of finding that position which is closest to the actual position (DR) of the observer. This is still the method we use today when solving for position graphically. St. Hilaire postulated that we need to assume a fictionalized position close to our DR. This Assumed Position yields a pre-calculated sextant altitude (Hc) that corresponds to that Assumed Position. We can then compare our actual sextant altitude (Ho) to the Hc, subtracting one from the other to find out if we are closer or further away from the GP of the celestial object. That's a lot of words to describe what we now call the Intercept Method.

Let's say it another way: The Intercept Method uses the difference between the sextant angle at the Assumed Position (Hc), which is tabulated, and the sextant angle that was recorded by the navigator at the DR (Ho). As a result of this method, HO249 and other sight reduction tables have evolved into the tabular books that we use today. These tables contain pre-calculated Hc and azimuth (Zn) values found from any number of Assumed Positions. In order to use the tables, the following arguments have to be met. These are a whole number of degrees of latitude and longitude that, when subtracted from the GHA (in west longitude, added in the east), gives a whole number of degrees to produce an LHA (Local Hour Angle) with no minutes and no tenths. This method is based on the difference between what the sextant angle Hc is at the Assumed Position and the sextant angle Ho, which is what the navigator recorded at his location.

More than any other aspect of learning celestial navigation, the concept of the Assumed Position sidelines all but the bravest. But don't let it throw you. Assumed Position is a method that was developed to simplify navigational tables. When using these tables, the Assumed Position is necessary. Some folks mistakenly think the Assumed Position is a made-up value, but it is not. The Assumed Position is predicated on the DR, a real value. HO249 and all the other tables tell us in essence where the GP of the sun is at a certain moment of time based on an Assumed Position. If the tables told us every possible DR, they would overwhelmingly be—someone has calculated—3,481 times larger than they are now, definitely not an easy collection of books to move around. So, to make the tables manageable, they are presented to the nearest degree of where a navigator believes the DR to be. So we must assume a position that corresponds to a whole degree both in latitude and LHA.

To enter the tables, we create an Assumed Position of a whole number of degrees of latitude, based on our DR latitude, and an LHA that is the result of an assumed longitude (based on our DR longitude) that when subtracted or added to our GHA gives a whole number of degrees with no minutes or tenths. We always use the Assumed Position as our starting point when we plot our LOP.

Any table we choose to use—whether HO249 or HO229—demands the same preliminary arguments. The Assumed Position, by the way—and it's important to remember this—is always based on the navigator's dead reckoning position. It is not a number that just comes out of thin air.

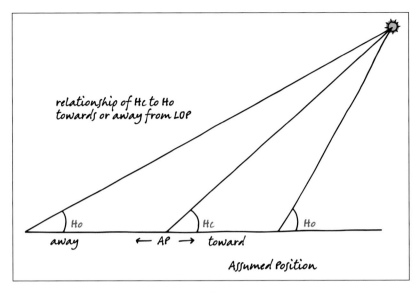

Intercept Diagram.

Since we already established the relationship between sextant angle and the distance from the GP in this first diagram, the Ho is greater than the Hc, so we must be closer by "X" to the GP. The rule to remember is Ho Mo To, which means Ho is more than the Hc, and toward the GP.

If the Hc is larger, as in the above diagram, then we are farther away. The distance we are either closer or farther away from the GP after we compare our Ho to the Hc is called the intercept. It is usually no more than a few miles, but—and this is important to remember—just because an intercept might be more than a few miles does not—I repeat, *does not*—mean that your observation or your calculations were incorrect. So do not assume that the length of the intercept diminishes the accuracy of your observation.

To Review:

So far, we have learned that we can find the GP of the sun for the exact moment of time by using the *Nautical Almanac* by finding the GHA and the declination. No matter what the sight reduction tables we use, the entering arguments will be the same. In order to calculate where we are, we need the following: a latitude of whole number of degrees, no minutes or tenths, an LHA that is a whole number of degrees no minutes or tenths, and a declination. Let's see how to derive these numbers. The assumed latitude is based on the DR latitude, so if the DR latitude is N 37°15' then the Assumed latitude will be N 37°. If the DR latitude is N 37°45', then the assumed latitude will be 38°. This just requires some thought; not much, just a bit.

The LHA has to be a whole number of degrees, so we create an assumed longitude so that when we subtract it from the GHA in west longitude or add in east longitude, we arrive at a whole number of degrees, no minutes or tenths. The assumed longitude is based on the DR longitude. The declination is found in the *Nautical Almanac* and should be rounded off to the nearest minute, thus a declination of S 17°18.6' would be S 17°19'. The sight reduction tables will only deal with minutes of declination and not tenths, so round up or down accordingly. We will delve into these tables in a moment.

All of this sounds cumbersome but will make sense after some practice. Just always remember that Assumed Position is based on the DR. It has to be created so that the entering arguments can be satisfied.

The sight reduction tables help solve the difficult math equations involved in celestial navigation, providing the user with accurate answers with a minimum of effort. The necessary spherical trigonometry has been pre-calculated, and set up in a tabular form that completely removes mathematical anxiety. The tables I prefer were developed for military transport pilots during the Second World War. Navigation was done celestially as planes were shipped across to Europe or the Far East and newly minted pilots required simple, compact, and accurate tables that could help them travel. Marine tables were too cumbersome for this, and so HO249 was developed and is actually called *Sight Reduction Tables for Air Navigation*. Don't be fooled; these tables are perfect for sailors.

There are many varieties of sight reduction tables. Use the ones that are the easiest and yield results with a minimum of hassle. Some people prefer HO229, or the earlier versions of HO214 or HO211. I am sold on the sight reduction tables labeled HO249. These tables are relatively simple to use, come in three volumes, two of which will last a lifetime. Crusty navigators will argue endlessly over the benefits of one set of sight reduction tables over another. Pay no attention. The ultimate accuracy of a celestial observation has much less to do with the sight reduction tables and much more on your ability with the sextant. Find what works and stay with it.

Once we have found the GHA of the sun we can then find our Local Hour Angle (LHA). This LHA is based on the DR longitude. Recall finding LHA in west longitude was done by subtracting west longitude from the GHA; that yields LHA. In order to use HO249, however, we need an LHA of a whole number of degrees with no minutes or tenths. Therefore, in order to use the tables, we create an assumed longitude, based on our DR longitude, so that when we subtract it from the GHA we get a whole number of degrees—no minutes or tenths that we can enter into HO249.

Let's continue.

On October 15, 2015 (see Page 48), we are at a DR of N 28°42' by W 58°15'. The time of the sextant observation, Hs, is at 10:38:38 GMT. Prepare information so we can enter HO249.

GHA at 1000 hours   333°32.1'   Dec. S 8°28.0'
38 minutes and 38 seconds   + 9°39.5'   (+d.09')   .6(.6')

The assumed longitude is based on the DR longitude of W 58°15'. We made the assumed longitude 58°53.4' so that when subtracted from the GHA of 342°53.4' we get results in degrees only and no minutes and no tenths.

GHA   343°11.6'   Dec. S 8°28.6'
− ass long   − (58°11.6')
LHA   285°

To use HO249, we need declination, which we now have, an LHA of a whole number of degrees with no minutes or tenths, which we now have, and a latitude of a whole degree called assumed latitude, which is based on our DR latitude. In this case the DR latitude was N 28°42', so our assumed latitude is 29°. It could also be 28°, but our resulting intercept will be longer. It is always best to go closest to the DR latitude when you assume latitude. The same goes for longitude as well, even if that means you move up to the next degree.

We will say more about HO249 soon, but for now it is important to see what is true. Number one, it is true that we can base an Assumed Position on our DR position. So we always basically know where we are. We have to create an Assumed Position so that we can use the sight reduction tables. Once we have an Assumed Position, if we are in western longitude, we can subtract that from the GHA so we get an LHA of a whole number of degrees no minutes and no tenths. Then we can use this to enter the tables. Our assumed latitude is based on the closest we can get, to a whole number of degrees, to our DR longitude. Don't overthink this. Just follow the procedure and after some practice it will begin to make sense. Let's do one more example.

It is October 14, 2015 (see page 48). We are at a DR of N 24°50' by W 83°18'. We take a sextant observation of the sun at 16 hrs, 38 min, 50 sec. We want to find the GP of the sun at the time of our observation. We also want to find the declination and the LHA. We also want to create an Assumed Position so that we can enter the sight reduction tables.

GHA at 1600 hours	63°29.5'	Dec S 8°11.4'
		+ (0.9) +.6
		Dec S 8° 10'
+38 min 50 sec	9°42.5'	*8° 12' ?*
GHA for time of sight	73°12.0'	

Okay, now we need to create an assumed longitude that will yield an LHA of degrees, no minutes and no tenths. The DR longitude is W 83°18', so we create an assumed longitude of W 83°12'.

GHA   73°12.0'
− ass long   83°12.0'

But we can not subtract a larger number from a smaller one, so we add 360° to the GHA (another circle) so we can mathematically proceed correctly thus.

GHA   73°12.0'
                     + 360°
GHA   433°12.0'
− ass long   83°12.0'
LHA   350°

Our DR latitude is N 24°50', so we create an assumed latitude of N 25° because that is closest to our DR latitude. We have our declination, our assumed latitude, and our LHA so we have enough information to enter the sight reduction tables.

Declination is S 8° 12'
Latitude is N 25°
GHA is 350°

2015 OCTOBER 13, 14, 15 (TUES., WED., THURS.)

UT	SUN GHA	Dec	MOON GHA	v	Dec	d	HP
13 00	183 23.6	S 7 34.0	182 48.1	14.9	S 6 01.1	8.8	54.0
01	198 23.7	35.0	197 22.0	14.9	6 09.9	8.7	54.1
02	213 23.9	35.9	211 55.9	14.9	6 18.6	8.7	54.1
03	228 24.0	.. 36.8	226 29.8	14.9	6 27.3	8.7	54.1
04	243 24.2	37.8	241 03.7	14.8	6 36.0	8.7	54.1
05	258 24.3	38.7	255 37.5	14.8	6 44.7	8.6	54.1
T 06	273 24.5	S 7 39.6	270 11.3	14.8	S 6 53.3	8.6	54.1
U 07	288 24.6	40.6	284 45.1	14.8	7 01.9	8.6	54.1
E 08	303 24.8	41.5	299 18.9	14.7	7 10.5	8.6	54.1
S 09	318 24.9	.. 42.5	313 52.6	14.7	7 19.1	8.5	54.1
D 10	333 25.1	43.4	328 26.3	14.7	7 27.6	8.5	54.1
A 11	348 25.2	44.3	343 00.0	14.7	7 36.1	8.4	54.1
Y 12	3 25.4	S 7 45.3	357 33.7	14.6	S 7 44.5	8.5	54.1
13	18 25.5	46.2	12 07.3	14.6	7 53.0	8.4	54.1
14	33 25.7	47.1	26 40.9	14.6	8 01.4	8.4	54.1
15	48 25.8	.. 48.1	41 14.5	14.5	8 09.8	8.3	54.1
16	63 26.0	49.0	55 48.0	14.6	8 18.1	8.3	54.2
17	78 26.1	49.9	70 21.6	14.5	8 26.4	8.3	54.2
18	93 26.3	S 7 50.9	84 55.1	14.4	S 8 34.7	8.2	54.2
19	108 26.4	51.8	99 28.5	14.5	8 42.9	8.3	54.2
20	123 26.6	52.7	114 02.0	14.4	8 51.2	8.1	54.2
21	138 26.7	.. 53.7	128 35.4	14.4	8 59.3	8.2	54.2
22	153 26.9	54.6	143 08.8	14.3	9 07.5	8.1	54.2
23	168 27.0	55.5	157 42.1	14.3	9 15.6	8.0	54.2
14 00	183 27.2	S 7 56.5	172 15.4	14.3	S 9 23.6	8.1	54.2
01	198 27.3	57.4	186 48.7	14.3	9 31.7	8.0	54.2
02	213 27.5	58.3	201 22.0	14.2	9 39.7	7.9	54.2
03	228 27.6	7 59.3	215 55.2	14.2	9 47.6	7.9	54.2
04	243 27.8	8 00.2	230 28.4	14.2	9 55.5	7.9	54.3
05	258 27.9	01.1	245 01.6	14.1	10 03.4	7.8	54.3
W 06	273 28.1	S 8 02.0	259 34.7	14.1	S10 11.2	7.8	54.3
E 07	288 28.2	03.0	274 07.8	14.1	10 19.0	7.8	54.3
D 08	303 28.4	03.9	288 40.9	14.0	10 26.8	7.7	54.3
N 09	318 28.5	.. 04.8	303 13.9	14.0	10 34.5	7.6	54.3
E 10	333 28.6	05.8	317 46.9	14.0	10 42.1	7.7	54.3
S 11	348 28.8	06.7	332 19.9	13.9	10 49.8	7.6	54.3
D 12	3 28.9	S 8 07.6	346 52.8	13.9	S10 57.3	7.6	54.3
A 13	18 29.1	08.6	1 25.7	13.8	11 04.9	7.5	54.3
Y 14	33 29.2	09.5	15 58.5	13.9	11 12.4	7.4	54.4
15	48 29.4	.. 10.4	30 31.4	13.7	11 19.8	7.4	54.4
16	63 29.5	11.4	45 04.1	13.8	11 27.2	7.3	54.4
17	78 29.7	12.3	59 36.9	13.7	11 34.5	7.3	54.4
18	93 29.8	S 8 13.2	74 09.6	13.7	S11 41.8	7.3	54.4
19	108 29.9	14.1	88 42.3	13.6	11 49.1	7.2	54.4
20	123 30.1	15.1	103 14.9	13.6	11 56.3	7.2	54.4
21	138 30.2	.. 16.0	117 47.5	13.6	12 03.5	7.1	54.4
22	153 30.4	16.9	132 20.1	13.5	12 10.6	7.0	54.4
23	168 30.5	17.9	146 52.6	13.5	12 17.6	7.0	54.5
15 00	183 30.7	S 8 18.8	161 25.1	13.5	S12 24.6	7.0	54.5
01	198 30.8	19.7	175 57.6	13.4	12 31.6	6.9	54.5
02	213 30.9	20.6	190 30.0	13.3	12 38.5	6.8	54.5
03	228 31.1	.. 21.6	205 02.3	13.4	12 45.3	6.8	54.5
04	243 31.2	22.5	219 34.7	13.3	12 52.1	6.7	54.5
05	258 31.4	23.4	234 07.0	13.2	12 58.8	6.7	54.5
T 06	273 31.5	S 8 24.3	248 39.2	13.3	S13 05.5	6.6	54.6
H 07	288 31.6	25.3	263 11.5	13.1	13 12.1	6.6	54.6
U 08	303 31.8	26.2	277 43.6	13.2	13 18.7	6.5	54.6
R 09	318 31.9	.. 27.1	292 15.8	13.1	13 25.2	6.4	54.6
S 10	333 32.1	28.0	306 47.9	13.0	13 31.6	6.4	54.6
D 11	348 32.2	29.0	321 19.9	13.0	13 38.0	6.4	54.6
A 12	3 32.3	S 8 29.9	335 51.9	13.0	S13 44.4	6.3	54.6
Y 13	18 32.5	30.8	350 23.9	13.0	13 50.7	6.2	54.7
14	33 32.6	31.7	4 55.9	12.8	13 56.9	6.1	54.7
15	48 32.8	.. 32.7	19 27.7	12.9	14 03.0	6.1	54.7
16	63 32.9	33.6	33 59.6	12.8	14 09.1	6.0	54.7
17	78 33.0	34.5	48 31.4	12.8	14 15.1	6.0	54.7
18	93 33.2	S 8 35.4	63 03.2	12.7	S14 21.1	5.9	54.7
19	108 33.3	36.4	77 34.9	12.7	14 27.0	5.9	54.7
20	123 33.5	37.3	92 06.6	12.6	14 32.9	5.7	54.7
21	138 33.6	.. 38.2	106 38.2	12.7	14 38.6	5.8	54.8
22	153 33.7	39.1	121 09.9	12.5	14 44.4	5.6	54.8
23	168 33.9	40.1	135 41.4	12.5	S14 50.0	5.6	54.8
	SD 16.1	d 0.9	SD 14.7		14.8		14.9

Twilight / Sunrise / Moonrise

Lat.	Naut.	Civil	Sunrise	Moonrise 13	14	15	16
N 72	04 49	06 07	07 17	07 34	09 09	10 49	12 34
N 70	04 54	06 04	07 07	07 23	08 51	10 21	11 51
68	04 57	06 02	06 59	07 14	08 37	10 00	11 22
66	05 00	05 59	06 52	07 07	08 25	09 44	11 00
64	05 02	05 57	06 46	07 00	08 16	09 31	10 43
62	05 04	05 55	06 40	06 55	08 08	09 19	10 29
60	05 06	05 54	06 36	06 51	08 01	09 10	10 17
N 58	05 07	05 52	06 32	06 47	07 54	09 02	10 07
56	05 08	05 51	06 28	06 43	07 49	08 54	09 58
54	05 09	05 49	06 25	06 40	07 44	08 48	09 50
52	05 09	05 48	06 22	06 37	07 40	08 42	09 43
50	05 10	05 47	06 20	06 34	07 36	08 37	09 37
45	05 10	05 44	06 14	06 29	07 27	08 25	09 23
N 40	05 10	05 42	06 09	06 24	07 20	08 16	09 12
35	05 10	05 39	06 05	06 20	07 14	08 08	09 02
30	05 09	05 37	06 01	06 16	07 08	08 01	08 54
20	05 06	05 32	05 54	06 10	06 59	07 49	08 40
N 10	05 03	05 27	05 48	06 05	06 51	07 38	08 27
0	04 58	05 22	05 43	06 00	06 43	07 29	08 15
S 10	04 51	05 16	05 37	05 55	06 36	07 19	08 04
20	04 42	05 08	05 31	05 49	06 28	07 08	07 51
30	04 31	04 59	05 24	05 43	06 19	06 56	07 37
35	04 23	04 54	05 19	05 40	06 14	06 50	07 29
40	04 14	04 47	05 15	05 36	06 08	06 42	07 20
45	04 02	04 39	05 09	05 31	06 01	06 33	07 09
S 50	03 48	04 29	05 02	05 26	05 53	06 22	06 56
52	03 41	04 24	04 59	05 24	05 49	06 17	06 50
54	03 33	04 18	04 56	05 21	05 45	06 12	06 43
56	03 23	04 13	04 52	05 18	05 40	06 06	06 35
58	03 13	04 06	04 48	05 15	05 35	05 59	06 27
S 60	03 00	03 58	04 43	05 11	05 30	05 51	06 17

Sunset / Twilight / Moonset

Lat.	Sunset	Civil	Naut.	Moonset 13	14	15	16
N 72	16 13	17 23	18 40	16 29	16 24	16 18	16 11
N 70	16 23	17 26	18 36	16 41	16 43	16 47	16 55
68	16 32	17 29	18 33	16 51	16 59	17 09	17 25
66	16 39	17 31	18 30	17 00	17 11	17 26	17 47
64	16 45	17 33	18 28	17 07	17 22	17 40	18 04
62	16 51	17 35	18 26	17 13	17 30	17 52	18 19
60	16 55	17 37	18 25	17 18	17 38	18 02	18 31
N 58	16 59	17 39	18 24	17 23	17 45	18 10	18 41
56	17 03	17 40	18 23	17 27	17 51	18 18	18 51
54	17 06	17 42	18 22	17 31	17 56	18 25	18 59
52	17 09	17 43	18 22	17 35	18 01	18 31	19 06
50	17 12	17 44	18 22	17 38	18 06	18 37	19 13
45	17 18	17 47	18 21	17 45	18 15	18 49	19 27
N 40	17 23	17 50	18 21	17 51	18 23	18 59	19 39
35	17 27	17 52	18 22	17 56	18 30	19 08	19 49
30	17 31	17 55	18 23	18 00	18 36	19 15	19 58
20	17 38	18 00	18 25	18 08	18 47	19 29	20 13
N 10	17 44	18 05	18 29	18 14	18 56	19 40	20 26
0	17 49	18 10	18 35	18 21	19 05	19 51	20 39
S 10	17 55	18 17	18 41	18 27	19 14	20 02	20 51
20	18 02	18 24	18 50	18 34	19 23	20 13	21 04
30	18 09	18 33	19 02	18 41	19 34	20 26	21 20
35	18 13	18 39	19 10	18 46	19 40	20 34	21 28
40	18 18	18 46	19 19	18 51	19 47	20 43	21 38
45	18 24	18 54	19 31	18 57	19 55	20 53	21 50
S 50	18 31	19 05	19 46	19 04	20 05	21 06	22 05
52	18 34	19 10	19 53	19 07	20 10	21 11	22 11
54	18 38	19 15	20 01	19 11	20 15	21 18	22 19
56	18 42	19 21	20 11	19 15	20 20	21 25	22 27
58	18 46	19 28	20 22	19 19	20 27	21 33	22 37
S 60	18 51	19 36	20 35	19 24	20 34	21 42	22 48

SUN / MOON

Day	Eqn. of Time 00h	12h	Mer. Pass.	Mer. Pass. Upper	Lower	Age	Phase
	m s	m s	h m	h m	h m	d	%
13	13 34	13 41	11 46	12 10	24 32	00	0
14	13 48	13 55	11 46	12 54	00 32	01	2
15	14 02	14 09	11 46	13 40	01 17	02	6

Increments and Corrections

38ᵐ

38 m	SUN PLANETS	ARIES	MOON	v or Corrⁿ d		v or Corrⁿ d		v or Corrⁿ d	
s	° '	° '	° '	' '		' '		' '	
00	9 30·0	9 31·6	9 04·0	0·0	0·0	6·0	3·9	12·0	7·7
01	9 30·3	9 31·8	9 04·3	0·1	0·1	6·1	3·9	12·1	7·8
02	9 30·5	9 32·1	9 04·5	0·2	0·1	6·2	4·0	12·2	7·8
03	9 30·8	9 32·3	9 04·7	0·3	0·2	6·3	4·0	12·3	7·9
04	9 31·0	9 32·6	9 05·0	0·4	0·3	6·4	4·1	12·4	8·0
05	9 31·3	9 32·8	9 05·2	0·5	0·3	6·5	4·2	12·5	8·0
06	9 31·5	9 33·1	9 05·5	0·6	0·4	6·6	4·2	12·6	8·1
07	9 31·8	9 33·3	9 05·7	0·7	0·4	6·7	4·3	12·7	8·1
08	9 32·0	9 33·6	9 05·9	0·8	0·5	6·8	4·4	12·8	8·2
09	9 32·3	9 33·8	9 06·2	0·9	0·6	6·9	4·4	12·9	8·3
10	9 32·5	9 34·1	9 06·4	1·0	0·6	7·0	4·5	13·0	8·3
11	9 32·8	9 34·3	9 06·7	1·1	0·7	7·1	4·6	13·1	8·4
12	9 33·0	9 34·6	9 06·9	1·2	0·8	7·2	4·6	13·2	8·5
13	9 33·3	9 34·8	9 07·1	1·3	0·8	7·3	4·7	13·3	8·5
14	9 33·5	9 35·1	9 07·4	1·4	0·9	7·4	4·7	13·4	8·6
15	9 33·8	9 35·3	9 07·6	1·5	1·0	7·5	4·8	13·5	8·7
16	9 34·0	9 35·6	9 07·9	1·6	1·0	7·6	4·9	13·6	8·7
17	9 34·3	9 35·8	9 08·1	1·7	1·1	7·7	4·9	13·7	8·8
18	9 34·5	9 36·1	9 08·3	1·8	1·2	7·8	5·0	13·8	8·9
19	9 34·8	9 36·3	9 08·6	1·9	1·2	7·9	5·1	13·9	8·9
20	9 35·0	9 36·6	9 08·8	2·0	1·3	8·0	5·1	14·0	9·0
21	9 35·3	9 36·8	9 09·0	2·1	1·3	8·1	5·2	14·1	9·0
22	9 35·5	9 37·1	9 09·3	2·2	1·4	8·2	5·3	14·2	9·1
23	9 35·8	9 37·3	9 09·5	2·3	1·5	8·3	5·3	14·3	9·2
24	9 36·0	9 37·6	9 09·8	2·4	1·5	8·4	5·4	14·4	9·2
25	9 36·3	9 37·8	9 10·0	2·5	1·6	8·5	5·5	14·5	9·3
26	9 36·5	9 38·1	9 10·2	2·6	1·7	8·6	5·5	14·6	9·4
27	9 36·8	9 38·3	9 10·5	2·7	1·7	8·7	5·6	14·7	9·4
28	9 37·0	9 38·6	9 10·7	2·8	1·8	8·8	5·6	14·8	9·5
29	9 37·3	9 38·8	9 11·0	2·9	1·9	8·9	5·7	14·9	9·6
30	9 37·5	9 39·1	9 11·2	3·0	1·9	9·0	5·8	15·0	9·6
31	9 37·8	9 39·3	9 11·4	3·1	2·0	9·1	5·8	15·1	9·7
32	9 38·0	9 39·6	9 11·7	3·2	2·1	9·2	5·9	15·2	9·8
33	9 38·3	9 39·8	9 11·9	3·3	2·1	9·3	6·0	15·3	9·8
34	9 38·5	9 40·1	9 12·1	3·4	2·2	9·4	6·0	15·4	9·9
35	9 38·8	9 40·3	9 12·4	3·5	2·2	9·5	6·1	15·5	9·9
36	9 39·0	9 40·6	9 12·6	3·6	2·3	9·6	6·2	15·6	10·0
37	9 39·3	9 40·8	9 12·9	3·7	2·4	9·7	6·2	15·7	10·1
38	9 39·5	9 41·1	9 13·1	3·8	2·4	9·8	6·3	15·8	10·1
39	9 39·8	9 41·3	9 13·3	3·9	2·5	9·9	6·4	15·9	10·2
40	9 40·0	9 41·6	9 13·6	4·0	2·6	10·0	6·4	16·0	10·3
41	9 40·3	9 41·8	9 13·8	4·1	2·6	10·1	6·5	16·1	10·3
42	9 40·5	9 42·1	9 14·1	4·2	2·7	10·2	6·5	16·2	10·4
43	9 40·8	9 42·3	9 14·3	4·3	2·8	10·3	6·6	16·3	10·5
44	9 41·0	9 42·6	9 14·5	4·4	2·8	10·4	6·7	16·4	10·5
45	9 41·3	9 42·8	9 14·8	4·5	2·9	10·5	6·7	16·5	10·6
46	9 41·5	9 43·1	9 15·0	4·6	3·0	10·6	6·8	16·6	10·7
47	9 41·8	9 43·3	9 15·2	4·7	3·0	10·7	6·9	16·7	10·7
48	9 42·0	9 43·6	9 15·5	4·8	3·1	10·8	6·9	16·8	10·8
49	9 42·3	9 43·8	9 15·7	4·9	3·1	10·9	7·0	16·9	10·8
50	9 42·5	9 44·1	9 16·0	5·0	3·2	11·0	7·1	17·0	10·9
51	9 42·8	9 44·3	9 16·2	5·1	3·3	11·1	7·1	17·1	11·0
52	9 43·0	9 44·6	9 16·4	5·2	3·3	11·2	7·2	17·2	11·0
53	9 43·3	9 44·8	9 16·7	5·3	3·4	11·3	7·3	17·3	11·1
54	9 43·5	9 45·1	9 16·9	5·4	3·5	11·4	7·3	17·4	11·2
55	9 43·8	9 45·3	9 17·2	5·5	3·5	11·5	7·4	17·5	11·2
56	9 44·0	9 45·6	9 17·4	5·6	3·6	11·6	7·4	17·6	11·3
57	9 44·3	9 45·8	9 17·6	5·7	3·7	11·7	7·5	17·7	11·4
58	9 44·5	9 46·1	9 17·9	5·8	3·7	11·8	7·6	17·8	11·4
59	9 44·8	9 46·4	9 18·1	5·9	3·8	11·9	7·6	17·9	11·5
60	9 45·0	9 46·6	9 18·4	6·0	3·9	12·0	7·7	18·0	11·6

The Sextant:
The Perfect Tool for the Job

Okay, so now that we have given a look to the tables, we are ready to finally begin discussing the sextant and what is necessary when using it to take an observation of the sun.

The sextant is a double-reflecting measuring tool designed to give the user the ability to see both the celestial object (sun) and the horizon simultaneously. It is the final result of hundreds of years of evolving instruments. It reached its perfection in the mind of Sir Isaac Newton, who is credited with its invention. Newton represented his idea for the double-reflecting mirrored tool to the Royal Academy in 1699. The idea was shelved until 1731 when English mathematician John Hadley began working on it. Interestingly enough, at the same time in Philadelphia, optician and amateur inventor Thomas Godfrey came up with the idea of a double-reflecting instrument. Godfrey was the one who ultimately received the prize from the Board of Longitude who adjudicated such matters, but it was Hadley's design that was ultimately implemented in manufacturing.

So the tool that you have in your hand is, historically speaking, not that old. It is worthwhile considering that by the time the great Age of Exploration was over, the sextant still was not born.

Like they say in the circus, it's all done with mirrors. Two, in this case. The index mirror is mounted perpendicular to the frame of the sextant and centered over a pivot point of the index arm. The second mirror is also perpendicular to the frame and is fixed so that it can reflect the image of the star from the object mirror into the observer's eye. The optical law of double-reflection explains why the scale of a sextant is calibrated to read twice the angle subtended by the object mirror. This law states that for a ray of light reflected from two mirrors in succession that the angles between the first and last direction of the light is twice the angle between the mirrors. Since the angle of the horizon mirror is fixed, the scale on the arc is constructed to read twice the angle of rotation of the index arm. That is why the sextant reads not 60° (1/6 of a circle) but 120°. The key point is that the path of a ray of light reflected from the index mirror is fixed by the geometry of the instrument and does not change when the mirror is rotated. The ray of light reflected by the index mirror is seen directly by the eye on the horizon mirror and then into the lens.

When the sextant was introduced, mariners who were used to using less-efficient tools like the cross-staff and the back-staff were loath to try it. The sextant finally gained acceptance when it was clear that it was so much more effective and easier to use. It ultimately achieved success because of its simplicity. The sextant is held vertically and pointed in the direction of the star while the observer looks directly at the horizon adjusting the index arm until the star comes into view. You don't have to turn your back to the sun as was necessary with the back-staff or look at both the horizon and the star as you did with the cross-staff.

A Short History of How We Arrived at the Sextant

Obviously, nothing comes out of thin air, and the sextant is the result of navigation tools that began with the human body. The ancients knew that the hand, the fingers extended, and the fist, all represent an arc of degrees. For instance, a closed fist held at arm's length is about 10° of arc. How do I know this? Well, if I make a fist and extend my arm out, placing my fist straight ahead at the horizon and again go up until it's right overhead, I will have moved my fist nine times. That would mean that directly overhead is 90°. Also, the distance from the thumb to the outstretched index finger is about 15°. The index finger held with the middle finger is about 5°. These are all with the arm stretched out. Even today these are valuable things to know. The Arabs coined a term called *issabah,* which is the angular measurement of an outstretched thumb equivalent to about 1.5°. Gradually, as mariners went further afield, more accurate means of making angular height measurements became necessary. Every culture with a maritime legacy participated in the development of more accurate navigational tools that could measure the height of a celestial object above the horizon. Most of the cultures north of the equator used Polaris, or the Pole Star, as the means of identifying latitude. The Arabic device called a kamal is perhaps the earliest expansion of measurement by fingers and hands. The kamal, sometimes referred to in modern times as "stick on a string," was made from a length of string connected to a piece of ivory or wood. The string was knotted in increments of one *issabah*. By observing the latitude of Polaris on leaving home, the Arab sailors could sail either north or south to the Malabar Coast across the Indian Ocean at the designated altitude. This, of course, is the origin of latitude sailing, a technique still used by celestial navigators today who can use the noon sight to ascertain latitude, or, as the Arabs did, Polaris.

Sextant Nomenclature

The field of vision provides a direct image on the left of the horizon and a reflected image on the right. By moving the index arm, an index mirror is rotated through a small angle. The celestial body is brought into coincidence with the horizon and the vertical angle is measured. When used on a moving vessel, the image of the horizon and the sun will move around the field of view. However, the relative positions will remain steady. When the sun touches the horizon, the accuracy of the measurement will be high compared to the magnitude of the movement.

Once you own a sextant you have to get accustomed to using it. As with all other skills, this requires practice. Of course, if you live on a sailboat, you can practice anytime. But for most others, practice requires finding an open space with an unobstructed horizon. The beach is perfect for this, but if you live in an urban location with buildings all around, you can practice with an inexpensive artificial horizon made by Davis Instruments (www.davisnet.com/product/artificial-horizon/). Working with an artificial horizon is good in a pinch, but it is far better to get to a place where you can replicate the experience you will encounter at sea. Of course, though, without bounding waves and sea spray.

A German-made sextant, the Plath, is considered the *sine qua non* amongst mariners. It is made of brass alloy, weighs about four pounds, and is truly an object of great beauty. Its heavy weight is favored by some navigators because it is very stable in high wind conditions, but others believe that holding the Plath is more akin to working out in a gym than doing celestial navigation. The Japanese are known for their aluminum alloy sextants, most notably the Tamaya, in models such as the Jupiter, the Spica, and Venus. These are beautiful tools and compare favorably with the Plath. These tools, when sold new, are close to the $2,000 price range. A very expensive investment unless one plans on doing a lot of long distance sailing. It should be said, though, that the ownership of one of these tools, like owning a piece of art, provides a great deal of pleasure even when it is not being used. On many cold winter days the contemplation of a beautifully-crafted sextant yields great joy; a sextant after all is not just a functioning tool, but also a pathway to escapism, which is not a bad thing.

Up until the 1980s the budding navigator had no way of purchasing a high-quality metal sextant for anything less than $1,500. That changed in 1986 when the Chinese began producing the Astra IIIb, a metal sextant that sold initially for about $400. To date there are more than 26,000 of these Astras worldwide.

The Astra IIIb sextant filled a niche and soon became very popular among students, teachers, and practicing navigators alike. Built of aluminum alloy, the Astra IIIb is light and holds up very well in all kinds of conditions. I own both a Plath and an Astra IIIb, but when teaching I never use my Plath at sea, as I want to share my sextants with the students. Understandably, I am much more willing to do that with a $400 sextant than a $2,000 sextant. Someone dropping my Astra would only elicit curses; someone dropping my Plath would be cause for mayhem. The Astra IIIb is a very good choice for any navigator. At today's prices they sell in the mid-$700 range, but can be found on eBay used. A note here about buying a used sextant: There is too much information concerning the sextant errors to be contained within this book. If you choose to buy a used sextant, I suggest that you also read Bruce Bauer's *The Sextant Handbook* (1986). Unless a sextant has been dropped or its mirrors have begun unsilvering, there is not really much that can go wrong with a used sextant. Again, though, buyer beware. Generally, sextants are sold in the used market after an owner has passed away, as very few sailors would ever sell their sextants, even if they were no longer sailing.

If you buy a used sextant, and there are many good values out there, familiarize yourself with prices and peruse eBay to get an idea of the market. Also be aware of sextants that are antique reproductions. Don't buy them if you plan to navigate. These sextants, and including any that are made completely of brass, are perfect for the fireplace mantel or the boardroom but are worthless at sea. Look for brand names like Plath, Friberger, Heath, and Tamaya. Stay away from aircraft bubble sextants, marine sextants that have an included artificial horizon, or those not name brand. Look for good silvering on the mirror. If there is a battery in the handle to light up the index arc, make certain that the light works and the battery box is not filled with corroded old batteries. Make sure the handle is secure to the frame. For checking the perpendicularity of the mirrors to the frame as well as other errors, again, please read *The Sextant Handbook*.

On the other hand, the plastic Davis sextants are very functional and worthy tools. The prices on the plastic high-end Davis sextants are close to $300, a not-inexpensive purchase for molded plastic. They are good tools, but you get what you pay for. I have used them many times and have not been unhappy. They do have a habit of racking in the heat and the index error has to be adjusted often, which fortunately on the Davis is not a difficult task. However, they have no aesthetic value and it is difficult to bond with a piece of plastic. They are serviceable tools, but for my money I would only use them in an emergency. Much better to use a tool of fine craftsmanship that will give some pleasure. The best resources for buying new sextants on site are probably Celestaire in Wichita, Kansas, Weems & Plath in Annapolis, Maryland, and Robert E. White Instruments in Boston, Massachusetts. Otherwise, put a notice in the local yacht club or in an associated Facebook group and see if you can find a used one. They are all over the place and there are good values out there. You just have to keep your eyes open.

Practicing with the Sextant

Once you own a sextant, you have to get accustomed to using it.

Like holding a baby, there is a right way to handle your sextant. The goal is to be gentle but firm. When passing a sextant to someone else, the phrase "got it?" is the one most heard. Some people believe a lanyard should be attached around the neck to hold the sextant. I personally think that is unnecessary and is just another thing that gets in the way. If you spend a few hundred dollars on a tool, you will be naturally careful.

Technique

Technique is always important, whether swinging a golf club, rowing a boat, or playing a guitar. This holds true for celestial navigation as well. In order to get the best observation of a celestial object, you should work on your technique. The classic method of celestial navigators is leaning against weather shrouds. When there is a sea running, the best thing is to sit in the main companionway hatch and make yourself comfortable. If the sun is hidden by the sails, you could ask your skipper to fall off the wind or head up a bit in order to allow you a good sight. If that is not possible, you could always trim in the headsail, back it, and heave to for a few moments. That will slow the boat down and give you a chance of not fighting too many things all at once. It is true that while sitting down, your height of eye will be reduced, but that change could be accommodated without too much trouble by using a nautical almanac, which we will get to later.

The process for taking an observation is always the same. You must always check the index error on the sextant; unless you have a plastic sextant or have dropped your more expensive metal sextant, the index error should not change. Nevertheless, it is still good protocol to check either at the beginning of or at the end of each observation. There are many methods of doing this, but the simplest is to set the index arm at 0° and the micrometer drum at 0' then look at the horizon. The reflected image of the horizon and the direct image should be a straight line.

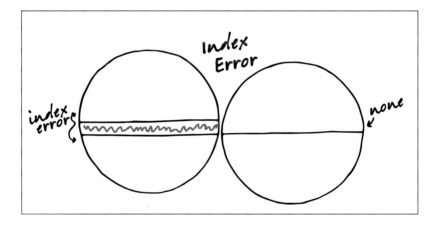

If it is not, adjust the micrometer drum until the horizon line lines up. The adjustment should only be a matter of a couple of minutes at most of arc. My Plath is usually off by two minutes of arc and that has remained constant over a long period of time. When using a plastic Davis sextant, it is very simple to use the gnarled screw holding the mirror in the index arm to set the sextant to 0° and thus eliminate any error. This will happen more often on plastic sextants as they are subject to variations in temperature. More often than not, on the higher-end metal sextants like the Astra IIIb or the Plath, the index error will usually be constant and so it will not need to be adjusted at all. Further, every sextant comes with wrenches that will adjust the mirrors. But I hesitate to have you do that just to zero out the error. As I said, if the index error remains constant, you are good to go. If you find the sextant is way out of whack, again, turn to *The Sextant Handbook*.

Once you have checked the index error, you are ready to take an observation. You must remember that when using the sextant, the sun's light is magnified to the point where it is easy to damage your eyes. The index mirror shades therefore are very important. There are three shades on the index mirror and a similar number on horizon mirrors. Best to begin with first and third on both and then see if you can see both the sun and the horizon. You want the horizon to be visible, but not too bright. Play around with this. If you see nothing, the sextant is not broken. It's just that you have too many shades in place. Obviously, the better the sextant, the higher quality of shades and lenses. So what works for one sextant may not be of value for another.

So now you are ready to take your sight. There are two schools of thought as to the best way to approach this. One school has it that you should set the sextant at 0°, 0', point it at the sun, then move the index arm until the sun is on the horizon. The other school says that you should estimate the height of the sun, set the index arm to that value, scan the sky until you see the sun, and then adjust the micrometer drum until the sun lowers to the horizon. This is actually easier than you think, as a closed fist held at arm's length is equivalent to about 10°. Before taking a sight, I measure, by using my fist, the approximate height of the sun in the sky, then I set my index arm to that angle. I never get it exactly, but it does minimize all the guesswork and you will be close enough to see the sun through the sextant and then fine-tune it with the micrometer. To perfect this practice, consult *The Stars by Clock and Fist* (1956) by Henry Neeley. As a beginner, one should practice this technique before even thinking about timing a shot. There is a considerable amount of hand-eye coordination required initially in using a sextant, but as with anything else, practice eliminates the uncertainty. The sextant should ultimately feel like an extension of your hand and not just like some hunk of metal that weighs a lot.

When taking this measurement, should you hold the sextant in your left hand and then use your left eye for observing? Or the right hand and right eye? Should you close one eye and keep one open? It all comes down to what feels most comfortable. I am of the belief that, if you can, it is better to keep both eyes open. This is easier than it sounds. (By the way, if you wear glasses, wear them when you are observing a celestial object.) And in order to practice I have used an eyepatch on my right eye in order to train it to stay open. I hold the sextant in my right hand and use my left eye, only because my vision is better in that eye. After practicing with my right eye open under the eye patch, I can keep my right eye open and see both the reflected image of the sun and the horizon outside the range of the sextant. This makes taking an accurate shot much easier. But perhaps I'm making too fine of a point. The most important thing is to be and feel comfortable and to take a great many sights as practice before you find a method that works for you. There are no rules here—just make sure that you are consistent and develop the confidence to know your observations are as accurate as possible. And now we are ready to take our first observation of the sun.

When you are ready to take a sun sight, here's what you should have done:

1. Checked index error.
2. Made certain the sun is higher in the sky than 10° (any less than that introduces extra refraction corrections that can influence the accuracy of the sight).
3. Be in possession of a watch that keeps accurate time (this is crucial as time is of the essence when it comes to celestial navigation).

Earth spins a full 360° in 24 hours. This is about 900 miles an hour at the equator. So this means an error in time of four seconds is equivalent to a matching error in the GP of the sun of one nautical mile. This might not sound critical in the middle of the ocean, but can be very critical when closing with land. Two centuries ago, keeping accurate time at sea was quite a challenge. In the mid-eighteenth century, English clockmaker John Harrison finally solved the problem with his No. 4 clock, which made calculating accurate longitude at sea infinitely easier. (A great read about this is *Longitude* [1955] by Dava Sobel.) It doesn't have to be spot on, but it is important that the clock must not lose or gain time. Not so long ago it was not uncommon before a passage to have chronometers calibrated prior to the voyage. This was very important to ascertain whether, over a period of time, the clocks would gain or lose time and this could be recorded. The clocks were wound a certain amount on a regular schedule. Now with battery-operated watches that's all become unnecessary.

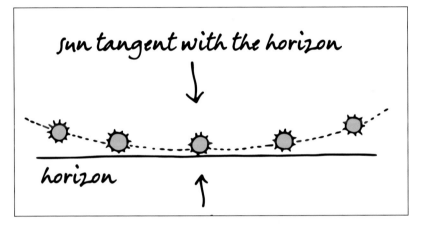

Also there are various hand-eye techniques that will be learned through the process of practice. Bowditch's *Practical American Navigator* is a good source of information for the best methods of practicing. But I will say the following just to touch upon the subject without getting too sidetracked. When taking a sight the sextant has to be rocked, that is, swung back and forth in a small arc so that the sun, when it is observed, it will be at its lowest point. It is confusing to describe, but when you think about it, it does makes sense. We want the sun to be perpendicular to the horizon when we take an observation. But, just because we are holding the sextant at what we think is a

A2 ALTITUDE CORRECTION TABLES 10°–90°—SUN,STARS,PLANETS

OCT.—MAR. SUN APR.—SEPT.						STARS AND PLANETS				DIP					
App. Alt.	Lower Limb	Upper Limb	App. Alt.	Lower Limb	Upper Limb	App. Alt.	Corrⁿ	App. Alt.	Additional Corrⁿ	Ht. of Eye	Corrⁿ	Ht. of Eye	Corrⁿ	Ht. of Eye	Corrⁿ

° ′			° ′			° ′		**2015**		m		ft.		m	
9 33	+10·8	−21·5	9 39	+10·6	−21·2	9 55	−5·3	**VENUS**		2·4	−2·8	8·0		1·0	−1·8
9 45	+10·9	−21·4	9 50	+10·7	−21·1	10 07	−5·2	Jan. 1–May 3		2·6	−2·9	8·6		1·5	−2·2
9 56	+11·0	−21·3	10 02	+10·8	−21·0	10 20	−5·1	Dec. 4–Dec. 31		2·8	−3·0	9·2		2·0	−2·5
10 08	+11·1	−21·2	10 14	+10·9	−20·9	10 32	−5·0	° ′		3·0	−3·1	9·8		2·5	−2·8
10 20	+11·2	−21·1	10 27	+11·0	−20·8	10 46	−4·9	60	+0·1	3·2	−3·2	10·5		3·0	−3·0
10 33	+11·3	−21·0	10 40	+11·1	−20·7	10 59	−4·8			3·4	−3·3	11·2		See table	
10 46	+11·4	−20·9	10 53	+11·2	−20·6	11 14	−4·7	May 4–June 22		3·6	−3·4	11·9		←	
11 00	+11·5	−20·8	11 07	+11·3	−20·5	11 29	−4·6	Oct. 13–Dec. 3		3·8	−3·5	12·6			
11 15	+11·6	−20·7	11 22	+11·4	−20·4	11 44	−4·5	° ′		4·0	−3·6	13·3		m	
11 30	+11·7	−20·6	11 37	+11·5	−20·3	12 00	−4·4	0	+0·2	4·3	−3·7	14·1		20	−7·9
11 45	+11·8	−20·5	11 53	+11·6	−20·2	12 17	−4·3	41	+0·1	4·5	−3·8	14·9		22	−8·3
12 01	+11·9	−20·4	12 10	+11·7	−20·1	12 35	−4·2	76		4·7	−3·9	15·7		24	−8·6
12 18	+12·0	−20·3	12 27	+11·8	−20·0	12 53	−4·1	June 23–July 14		5·0	−4·0	16·5		26	−9·0
12 36	+12·1	−20·2	12 45	+11·9	−19·9	13 12	−4·0	Sept. 19–Oct. 12		5·2	−4·1	17·4		28	−9·3
12 54	+12·2	−20·1	13 04	+12·0	−19·8	13 32	−3·9	° ′		5·5	−4·2	18·3			
13 14	+12·3	−20·0	13 24	+12·1	−19·7	13 53	−3·8	0	+0·3	5·8	−4·3	19·1		30	−9·6
13 34	+12·4	−19·9	13 44	+12·2	−19·6	14 16	−3·7	34	+0·2	6·1	−4·4	20·1		32	−10·0
13 55	+12·5	−19·8	14 06	+12·3	−19·5	14 39	−3·6	60	+0·1	6·3	−4·5	21·0		34	−10·3
14 17	+12·6	−19·7	14 29	+12·4	−19·4	15 03	−3·5	80		6·6	−4·6	22·0		36	−10·6
14 41	+12·7	−19·6	14 53	+12·5	−19·3	15 29	−3·4	July 15–July 30		6·9	−4·7	22·9		38	−10·8
15 05	+12·8	−19·5	15 18	+12·6	−19·2	15 56	−3·3	Sept. 2–Sept. 18		7·2	−4·8	23·9			
15 31	+12·9	−19·4	15 45	+12·7	−19·1	16 25	−3·2	° ′		7·5	−4·9	24·9		40	−11·1
15 59	+13·0	−19·3	16 13	+12·8	−19·0	16 55	−3·1	0	+0·4	7·9	−5·0	26·0		42	−11·4
16 27	+13·1	−19·2	16 43	+12·9	−18·9	17 27	−3·0	29	+0·3	8·2	−5·1	27·1		44	−11·7
16 58	+13·2	−19·1	17 14	+13·0	−18·8	18 01	−2·9	51	+0·2	8·5	−5·2	28·1		46	−11·9
17 30	+13·3	−19·0	17 47	+13·1	−18·7	18 37	−2·8	68	+0·1	8·8	−5·3	29·2		48	−12·2
18 05	+13·4	−18·9	18 23	+13·2	−18·6	19 16	−2·7	83		9·2	−5·4	30·4			
18 41	+13·5	−18·8	19 00	+13·3	−18·5	19 56	−2·6	July 31–Sept. 1		9·5	−5·5	31·5		ft.	
19 20	+13·6	−18·7	19 41	+13·4	−18·4	20 40	−2·5	° ′		9·9	−5·6	32·7		2	−1·4
20 02	+13·7	−18·6	20 24	+13·5	−18·3	21 27	−2·4	0	+0·5	10·3	−5·7	33·9		4	−1·9
20 46	+13·8	−18·5	21 10	+13·6	−18·2	22 17	−2·3	26	+0·4	10·6	−5·8	35·1		6	−2·4
21 34	+13·9	−18·4	21 59	+13·7	−18·1	23 11	−2·2	46	+0·3	11·0	−5·9	36·3		8	−2·7
22 25	+14·0	−18·3	22 52	+13·8	−18·0	24 09	−2·1	60	+0·2	11·4	−6·0	37·6		10	−3·1
23 20	+14·1	−18·2	23 49	+13·9	−17·9	25 12	−2·0	73	+0·1	11·8	−6·1	38·9		See table	
24 20	+14·2	−18·1	24 51	+14·0	−17·8	26 20	−1·9	84		12·2	−6·2	40·1		←	
25 24	+14·3	−18·0	25 58	+14·1	−17·7	27 34	−1·8	**MARS**		12·6	−6·3	41·5		ft.	
26 34	+14·4	−17·9	27 11	+14·2	−17·6	28 54	−1·7	Jan. 1–Dec. 31		13·0	−6·4	42·8		70	−8·1
27 50	+14·5	−17·8	28 31	+14·3	−17·5	30 22	−1·6	° ′		13·4	−6·5	44·2		75	−8·4
29 13	+14·6	−17·7	29 58	+14·4	−17·4	31 58	−1·5	0	+0·1	13·8	−6·6	45·5		80	−8·7
30 44	+14·7	−17·6	31 33	+14·5	−17·3	33 43	−1·4	60		14·2	−6·7	46·9		85	−8·9
32 24	+14·8	−17·5	33 18	+14·6	−17·2	35 38	−1·3			14·7	−6·8	48·4		90	−9·2
34 15	+14·9	−17·4	35 15	+14·7	−17·1	37 45	−1·2			15·1	−6·9	49·8		95	−9·5
36 17	+15·0	−17·3	37 24	+14·8	−17·0	40 06	−1·1			15·5	−7·0	51·3		100	−9·7
38 34	+15·1	−17·2	39 48	+14·9	−16·9	42 42	−1·0			16·0	−7·1	52·8		105	−9·9
41 06	+15·2	−17·1	42 28	+15·0	−16·8	45 34	−0·9			16·5	−7·2	54·3		110	−10·2
43 56	+15·3	−17·0	45 29	+15·1	−16·7	48 45	−0·8			16·9	−7·3	55·8		115	−10·4
47 07	+15·4	−16·9	48 52	+15·2	−16·6	52 16	−0·7			17·4	−7·4	57·4		120	−10·6
50 43	+15·5	−16·8	52 41	+15·3	−16·5	56 09	−0·6			17·9	−7·5	58·9		125	−10·8
54 46	+15·6	−16·7	56 59	+15·4	−16·4	60 26	−0·5			18·4	−7·6	60·5			
59 21	+15·7	−16·6	61 50	+15·5	−16·3	65 06	−0·4			18·8	−7·7	62·1		130	−11·1
64 28	+15·8	−16·5	67 15	+15·6	−16·2	70 09	−0·3			19·3	−7·8	63·8		135	−11·3
70 10	+15·9	−16·4	73 14	+15·7	−16·1	75 32	−0·2			19·8	−7·9	65·4		140	−11·5
76 24	+16·0	−16·3	79 42	+15·8	−16·0	81 12	−0·1			20·4	−8·0	67·1		145	−11·7
83 05	+16·1	−16·2	86 31	+15·9	−15·9	87 03	0·0			20·9	−8·1	68·8		150	−11·9
90 00			90 00			90 00				21·4		70·5		155	−12·1

App. Alt. = Apparent altitude = Sextant altitude corrected for index error and dip.

Example of A2 Altitude and Correction Table.

perpendicular angle does not make it so. Remember that you are most likely on a bouncing, heeling boat, so by rocking the sextant we can actually visually find the lowest spot where we are perpendicular. It sometimes feels a bit out of whack, but it is correct.

Since the goal here is to learn the basics of celestial navigation without getting too bogged down, I have intentionally omitted a discussion about time zones. If you're interested, however, time zones make for a very interesting subject. Bowditch is an excellent reference should you want to engage further. Suffice it to say that since the apparent sun is moving at 15° every hour, every time zone is at a 15° increment. Celestial navigation is based on time at the Greenwich meridian 0° longitude, or GHA 0° on the celestial sphere. Again, the navigator's watch should always be set to Greenwich Mean Time, since observations of the sun are recorded in Greenwich Mean Time. It's best to set your watch to Greenwich Time, so as to avoid confusion.

When you take an observation of the sun, the recorded numbers of the observation are labeled Hs (sextant altitude). This Hs needs to be refined to yield a Ho (observed altitude), which is the value that you are seeking. Remember, the premise is that you are at the center of the earth when you take an observation. So you have to include corrections to the Hs in order to mathematically create being at the center of the earth without, thank goodness, actually being there.

In the diagram on the previous page, we are interested in the sun tables to the left side of the page and the dip tables to the right side. You will notice that the dip tables are listed as both meters (m) and feet (ft). These tables are referred to as critical tables, which means that the two numbers together refer to one solution. For instance, at the top of the table height of eye between 8 feet and 8.6 feet has a dip correction of -2.8 minutes (the table is in minutes and tenths, not degrees, minutes, and tenths). Between 8.6 feet and 9.2 feet, the correction is -2.9 minutes and so on. For the sake of argument, let's say that a height of eye is 10 feet. Go down the column until you see 9.8 feet and 10.5 feet. The dip correction that refers to both numbers is -3.1 minutes. This correction now has to be brought into the process of reducing the sight. For this exercise, let's say it is October, any day, and the sextant observation of the sun is Hs 35° 27.5'. We are observing the lower limb. The time and date are not important for this exercise. In this example there is no index error.

Hs	35° 27.5'
– Dip	3.1'
App Alt	35° 24.4'

This number is then labeled as App alt. You now have to add three more corrections in order to refine our sights. Remember the SD, or semi-diameter, we spoke of earlier? The other two corrections are parallax and refraction. Both parallax and refraction are associated with the bending of the sun's light. Refraction is a vertical bending and parallax is a horizontal. Both parallax and refraction are dependent on the altitude of the observation and the distance of the sun. Remember, as we discussed before, the earth is an elliptical orbit around the sun. There are times of the year when the sun is closer, thus making the SD larger, and times when it is farther away, making it smaller. All three corrections—SD, parallax, and refraction—are folded into one great correction, appropriately called—what else?—third correction.

Under the sun correction column, you will see the following columns: App alt, Lower Limb, and Upper Limb. Above these are the months October to March and April to September. This labeling refers to the time of the year of the observation. As we have already established, the distance from the earth to the sun is always changing. If you happen to make a mistake here, it is not that critical. But always look under the correct column for the sake of accuracy.

So with the subtraction of the dip correction, we know that our App alt is 35° 24.4'. Go down the column for October to March, lower limb, under App alt, until you reach the number 34° 15'. Between this number and the next of 36° 17' that the third correction for the lower limb sight is +14.9'. Now think about that for a moment. If we are taking a sight of the lower limb of the sun, and we are attempting to find the mathematical center of the sun, it makes sense to add the third correction. You will notice by looking at the table that the upper limb correction is subtracted.

Always pay close attention here, as it is easy to make a careless mistake.

So now we have the following: Hs 35° 27.5' minus dip of 3.1 gives us apparent altitude of 35° 24.4', plus the third correction of 14.9' equals HO of 35° 39.3'.

This is the standard operating procedure for sight reduction. The sextant, the Hs, is of no value unless the sight is reduced, factoring in the index error, dip correction, parallax, refraction, and semi-diameter. We always use the final number, called Ho, or observed sextant altitude, to compare with the Hc that we will get from the tables.

Hs	35°	27.5'
dip*	–	3.1
app alt	35°	24.4'
3rd corr	+	14.9'
Ho	35°	39.3'

* dip is always subtracted

Let's do another example:

Hs is 52° 35.6'. Height of eye is 15 feet. The month the observation is taken is April. This time, we are taking an upper limb observation of the sun. The index error on the sextant is +.02', which means that the sextant is reading high .02'. Not unlike a ruler that is starting at ½ inch instead of 0, when the index error is high, or on the arc, it must be subtracted from the Hs. Similarly, when the index error is low, or off the arc, it must be added to the Hs. The mnemonic you can remember is the following: When you are on you are off, and when you are off, you are on. Confusing enough? Now let's find the Ho from the Hs.

	Hs	52°	35.6'
index cor	-		-.2'
dip	-		3.8'
appalt		52°	31.6°
3rd corr	-	16.6' (upper limb)	
Ho	52°	15.0'	

One thing I should add that may make your lives easier. This might sound like blasphemy to some, but I would say that you can just record your sextant altitude in degrees and minutes and round off the tenths on the micrometer drum. Remember that each minute of arc is equivalent to one nautical mile; therefore, three-tenths of the micrometer drum is only three tenths of a nautical mile. I would round that down and round tenths over six to the nearest minute.

So now that you have some understanding of what is going on when using celestial navigation, it's time to put all this information together and practice.

You can't, of course, replicate the actual taking of a celestial observation while aboard a boat, but you can, in the comfort of our dry, nonmoving homes on land, practice the procedures that will allow you to find position. Remember, practice is just that. It means going over the techniques slowly and methodically, so that after some time you fully understand the process.

You will always need the same tools on deck every time you prepare to take an observation: a watch that is set to

GMT, a pad, a pencil, and a sextant. A note here about watch time: I always have a digital wristwatch that is set to GMT. Usually, a ship's clock will be set to zone time, but the watch that I wear and take sights with is always set to GMT. I check it either after or before taking a sight with either a radio time check or by checking the time on the GPS. Most sailors will get their time from their GPS, but there is an offset between GPS time and universal time that can be as great as eight seconds. Usually, with GPS units installed on board, this is compensated for, but on less expensive handheld units one should read the manual to see what the time difference is. If there is a single sideband radio, there are time ticks given on 10 MGH or 5 MGH, or 15 or 20 MGH from Fort Collins, Colorado. The stations listed would be WWV and WWVH. The time tick is provided by the National Weather Service. WWV comes from Fort Collins, and WWVH from Hawaii.

The great revolution in accurate, inexpensive watches over the last decades has been a boon to celestial navigators. A digital quartz watch costing less than fifty dollars is more accurate than any marine chronometer that required winding up. I advise not to use your precious Rolex, though. It is more accurate to use a digital watch, and since timekeeping is so essential, keep your navigation watch in a safe place, until you are ready to take a sight. The pad, by the way, should be small enough to put in your back pocket and the pencil should be sharp enough so you can write with it.

Usually during the course of a day, the celestial navigator will do a series of three sun sights, one in the early morning, then a noon sight, and then a sight later in the afternoon.

These three observations will produce lines of position and we like to have intersections—or good cuts—of our LOPs. So we like to take sights every three hours or so. Remember that the apparent sun is moving at 15° an hour, so three hours gives us a cut of 45°. Of course, you could take sights any time you choose.

It is necessary to know the position, or DR, of the vessel at about the time the observation is taken. If you have been in charge of the plotting, then you generally have a good idea of where you are. You don't have to be exactly at the DR, which after all is just an educated guess anyway; as long as you are within fifty miles or so of it, you are good to go.

You need to remember to check the index error on the sextant each and every time you use it. If it is a good metal sextant, either of brass or aluminum, it is unlikely that the index error will change, but it's a good idea to get into the habit of checking it. If your index error is high, it will be subtracted; if it is low, it is added. You can work with index error as it is factored into the calculations and it should never be more than a few minutes of arc.

Okay. Now we're ready to pretend we are out at sea on a calm day with plenty of sunshine and blue sky. It's June 5 and according to the chart, the DR is 40°25' N by 68°15' W. (See table on page 76.) You want to take an observation of the lower limb of the sun. Sextant in hand, you position yourself on the deck on the windward side of the boat. You check your index error by sighting the horizon and getting the sextant to 0°0'. If the direct image and the reflected image line up, there is no index error. If the micrometer drum needs to be readjusted to get that image in a straight line, do so, and see if the adjustment is positive or negative. In other words, if it is On the Arc or Off the Arc. If it is On the Arc, then you subtract the minutes or tenths of minutes read on the micrometer drum, and if it is Off the Arc, you add ("If you are on, you're off; if you're off, you're on.") Then record it. Usually, the index error will remain constant. For this first exercise, let us assume that there is no index error.

With sunshades in place so that you don't get blinded, sight the lower limb of the sun. Take your observation and immediately check your watch. Let's say that the time of the observation was 13:56:10 GMT. Then write down your sextant angle. Do this carefully and slowly to avoid error. Then take another shot, record it, and then another. One way to know if you are on the right track is that since it is before noon, the sun should be rising. So every later shot the sun should be just a tad higher in the sky. If it is not, check your sextant readings.

There are different schools of thought concerning what should be done with these numbers. Some say they should be averaged. In other words, the three times should be averaged and the three sextant observations should be averaged. But I always take the middle sight and use that. Either way, do what makes you happiest. It doesn't take long to average the sight, but it is another place where mistakes could crop up; it's just as easy to choose the middle sight and then use that. And don't forget when you mark the time, to write the seconds first, then minutes and hours.

So, we have taken three sights and I am going to use the middle shot with an Hs of 42°6'.00 and a time of 13:56:10 GMT. Fold back the mirrors of the sextant, the sunshades, go below deck, and clean off the sextant if it got sprayed with salt water, and put it away. Now for the books. Find a comfortable seat and take out your *Nautical Almanac* and your sight reduction tables. (In this book, I only use HO249.) Hs at 13:56:10 is 42°06′. Once we are comfortable down below, we need the two books that will convert our Hs into position. These are the marine version of the *Nautical Almanac* and Volume III, HO249, for latitudes 39 to 89, and declinations from 0° to 29°.

Open the *Nautical Almanac* to the sun pages, June 5 (page 76). Look under the left-hand column labeled "Sun GHA." Go down the column of UT (to the very left) to 1300 hours and write down the GHA in declination. GHA at 1300 hours is 15°23.3′. The Declination is N 22°32.5′. It is essential to make certain that you mark the degrees, minutes, and tenths of declination correctly. The sign of the declination is marked as either N or S at 00, 06, 012, or 018 hours. To make certain that you understand this, notice that the declination for 1400 hours is increasing by .3′. It is N 22°32.8′. Think about this and it should make perfect sense as the declination of the sun increases until June 21 when we reach the summer solstice.

So now we have the GHA and declination for 1300 hours. That's great. But we took our shot at 13:56:10. We need to find out how far the apparent sun has moved and we need to find the GHA and declination for exactly the time we took our observation. Here's what to do.

Flip towards the end of the *Nautical Almanac* to the Increments and Corrections table and find the page of 56 minutes (page 74). You will see three columns labeled "Sun/ Planets," "Aries," "Moon," and another three columns with "v" or d corrections.

56^m

56 m	SUN PLANETS	ARIES	MOON	v or d	Corr^n	v or d	Corr^n	v or d	Corr^n
s	° ′	° ′	° ′	′	′	′	′	′	′
00	14 00·0	14 02·3	13 21·7	0·0	0·0	6·0	5·7	12·0	11·3
01	14 00·3	14 02·6	13 22·0	0·1	0·1	6·1	5·7	12·1	11·4
02	14 00·5	14 02·8	13 22·2	0·2	0·2	6·2	5·8	12·2	11·5
03	14 00·8	14 03·1	13 22·4	0·3	0·3	6·3	5·9	12·3	11·6
04	14 01·0	14 03·3	13 22·7	0·4	0·4	6·4	6·0	12·4	11·7
05	14 01·3	14 03·6	13 22·9	0·5	0·5	6·5	6·1	12·5	11·8
06	14 01·5	14 03·8	13 23·2	0·6	0·6	6·6	6·2	12·6	11·9
07	14 01·8	14 04·1	13 23·4	0·7	0·7	6·7	6·3	12·7	12·0
08	14 02·0	14 04·3	13 23·6	0·8	0·8	6·8	6·4	12·8	12·1
09	14 02·3	14 04·6	13 23·9	0·9	0·8	6·9	6·5	12·9	12·1
10	14 02·5	14 04·8	13 24·1	1·0	0·9	7·0	6·6	13·0	12·2
11	14 02·8	14 05·1	13 24·4	1·1	1·0	7·1	6·7	13·1	12·3
12	14 03·0	14 05·3	13 24·6	1·2	1·1	7·2	6·8	13·2	12·4
13	14 03·3	14 05·6	13 24·8	1·3	1·2	7·3	6·9	13·3	12·5
14	14 03·5	14 05·8	13 25·1	1·4	1·3	7·4	7·0	13·4	12·6
15	14 03·8	14 06·1	13 25·3	1·5	1·4	7·5	7·1	13·5	12·7
16	14 04·0	14 06·3	13 25·6	1·6	1·5	7·6	7·2	13·6	12·8
17	14 04·3	14 06·6	13 25·8	1·7	1·6	7·7	7·3	13·7	12·9
18	14 04·5	14 06·8	13 26·0	1·8	1·7	7·8	7·3	13·8	13·0
19	14 04·8	14 07·1	13 26·3	1·9	1·8	7·9	7·4	13·9	13·1
20	14 05·0	14 07·3	13 26·5	2·0	1·9	8·0	7·5	14·0	13·2
21	14 05·3	14 07·6	13 26·7	2·1	2·0	8·1	7·6	14·1	13·3
22	14 05·5	14 07·8	13 27·0	2·2	2·1	8·2	7·7	14·2	13·4
23	14 05·8	14 08·1	13 27·2	2·3	2·2	8·3	7·8	14·3	13·5
24	14 06·0	14 08·3	13 27·5	2·4	2·3	8·4	7·9	14·4	13·6
25	14 06·3	14 08·6	13 27·7	2·5	2·4	8·5	8·0	14·5	13·7
26	14 06·5	14 08·8	13 27·9	2·6	2·4	8·6	8·1	14·6	13·7
27	14 06·8	14 09·1	13 28·2	2·7	2·5	8·7	8·2	14·7	13·8
28	14 07·0	14 09·3	13 28·4	2·8	2·6	8·8	8·3	14·8	13·9
29	14 07·3	14 09·6	13 28·7	2·9	2·7	8·9	8·4	14·9	14·0
30	14 07·5	14 09·8	13 28·9	3·0	2·8	9·0	8·5	15·0	14·1
31	14 07·8	14 10·1	13 29·1	3·1	2·9	9·1	8·6	15·1	14·2
32	14 08·0	14 10·3	13 29·4	3·2	3·0	9·2	8·7	15·2	14·3
33	14 08·3	14 10·6	13 29·6	3·3	3·1	9·3	8·8	15·3	14·4
34	14 08·5	14 10·8	13 29·8	3·4	3·2	9·4	8·9	15·4	14·5
35	14 08·8	14 11·1	13 30·1	3·5	3·3	9·5	8·9	15·5	14·6
36	14 09·0	14 11·3	13 30·3	3·6	3·4	9·6	9·0	15·6	14·7
37	14 09·3	14 11·6	13 30·6	3·7	3·5	9·7	9·1	15·7	14·8
38	14 09·5	14 11·8	13 30·8	3·8	3·6	9·8	9·2	15·8	14·9
39	14 09·8	14 12·1	13 31·0	3·9	3·7	9·9	9·3	15·9	15·0
40	14 10·0	14 12·3	13 31·3	4·0	3·8	10·0	9·4	16·0	15·1
41	14 10·3	14 12·6	13 31·5	4·1	3·9	10·1	9·5	16·1	15·2
42	14 10·5	14 12·8	13 31·8	4·2	4·0	10·2	9·6	16·2	15·3
43	14 10·8	14 13·1	13 32·0	4·3	4·0	10·3	9·7	16·3	15·3
44	14 11·0	14 13·3	13 32·2	4·4	4·1	10·4	9·8	16·4	15·4
45	14 11·3	14 13·6	13 32·5	4·5	4·2	10·5	9·9	16·5	15·5
46	14 11·5	14 13·8	13 32·7	4·6	4·3	10·6	10·0	16·6	15·6
47	14 11·8	14 14·1	13 32·9	4·7	4·4	10·7	10·1	16·7	15·7
48	14 12·0	14 14·3	13 33·2	4·8	4·5	10·8	10·2	16·8	15·8
49	14 12·3	14 14·6	13 33·4	4·9	4·6	10·9	10·3	16·9	15·9
50	14 12·5	14 14·8	13 33·7	5·0	4·7	11·0	10·4	17·0	16·0
51	14 12·8	14 15·1	13 33·9	5·1	4·8	11·1	10·5	17·1	16·1
52	14 13·0	14 15·3	13 34·1	5·2	4·9	11·2	10·5	17·2	16·2
53	14 13·3	14 15·6	13 34·4	5·3	5·0	11·3	10·6	17·3	16·3
54	14 13·5	14 15·8	13 34·6	5·4	5·1	11·4	10·7	17·4	16·4
55	14 13·8	14 16·1	13 34·9	5·5	5·2	11·5	10·8	17·5	16·5
56	14 14·0	14 16·3	13 35·1	5·6	5·3	11·6	10·9	17·6	16·6
57	14 14·3	14 16·6	13 35·3	5·7	5·4	11·7	11·0	17·7	16·7
58	14 14·5	14 16·8	13 35·6	5·8	5·5	11·8	11·1	17·8	16·8
59	14 14·8	14 17·1	13 35·8	5·9	5·6	11·9	11·2	17·9	16·9
60	14 15·0	14 17·3	13 36·1	6·0	5·7	12·0	11·3	18·0	17·0

Go down the column of 56 minutes until you reach 10 seconds. Remember, our observation was at 13:56:10. Look under the "Sun/Planets" column and find the number 14°02.5'. This number means the following: that in 56 minutes and 13 seconds the apparent sun has moved 14°02.5' in a westerly direction, which makes sense since we have already established that the apparent sun is moving at 15° an hour.

Copy this number down. This will be added to the GHA. Now moving on to the declination. That too is changing, albeit much more slowly, and is moving in a northerly direction in 56 minutes. But by how much? Remember that declination in the celestial sphere corresponds to latitude on land. So in order to find the exact GP of the celestial object, we need to fix this position at the exact moment of our observation.

Go back to the June 5 sun pages in the *Nautical Almanac* (page 76) and notice at the bottom of the page under the sun column are two numbers. One is labeled SD, for the semi-diameter of the sun; it plays no importance in our calculations. The other number, labeled d, is, in this case, 0.3'. This means that at this time of year the declination of the sun is changing at .3' every hour, or .3 Nautical Miles per hour. This change needs to be calculated into the declination.

Back at the 56' page of Increments and Corrections, look under the "v" or d columns. We look at the small-numbered left column and see that the d correction of .3 corresponds to a larger number .3. This says that in 56 minutes the sun has moved 0.3'. Now do we add or subtract this from the declination? We know from observation of the tables that the declination is increasing every hour, so

2015 JUNE 3, 4, 5 (WED., THURS., FRI.)   113

UT	SUN GHA	SUN Dec	MOON GHA	MOON v	MOON Dec	MOON d	MOON HP	Lat.	Twilight Naut.	Twilight Civil	Sunrise	Moonrise 3	Moonrise 4	Moonrise 5	Moonrise 6
d h	° ′	° ′	° ′	′	° ′	′		°	h m	h m	h m	h m	h m	h m	h m
3 00	180 29.7	N22 14.5	355 44.8	8.6	S18 02.1	2.2	57.2	N 72	▭	▭	▭	■■■	01 34	01 10	
01	195 29.6	14.8	10 12.4	8.6	18 04.3	2.1	57.2	N 70	▭	▭	▭	23 38	24 14	00 14	00 29
02	210 29.5	15.1	24 40.0	8.5	18 06.4	2.0	57.2	68	////	////	01 01	22 52	23 35	24 00	00 00
03	225 29.4	.. 15.5	39 07.5	8.5	18 08.4	1.9	57.2	66	////	////	01 52	22 22	23 08	23 39	24 00
04	240 29.3	15.8	53 35.0	8.4	18 10.3	1.8	57.3	64	////	////	02 23	21 59	22 47	23 22	23 47
05	255 29.2	16.1	68 02.4	8.4	18 12.1	1.7	57.3	62	////	01 19	02 46	21 41	22 30	23 08	23 37
06	270 29.1	N22 16.4	82 29.8	8.3	S18 13.8	1.6	57.3	60	////	01 55	03 04	21 26	22 16	22 56	23 27
W 07	285 29.0	16.7	96 57.1	8.4	18 15.4	1.4	57.3	N 58	////	02 21	03 19	21 14	22 04	22 45	23 19
E 08	300 28.9	17.0	111 24.5	8.2	18 16.8	1.4	57.4	56	01 12	02 41	03 33	21 03	21 54	22 36	23 12
D 09	315 28.8	.. 17.3	125 51.7	8.3	18 18.2	1.3	57.4	54	01 46	02 57	03 44	20 53	21 44	22 28	23 05
N 10	330 28.7	17.6	140 19.0	8.2	18 19.5	1.1	57.4	52	02 09	03 11	03 54	20 44	21 36	22 21	23 00
E 11	345 28.6	17.9	154 46.2	8.2	18 20.6	1.1	57.4	50	02 51	03 39	04 15	20 37	21 29	22 15	22 54
S 12	0 28.5	N22 18.2	169 13.4	8.1	S18 21.7	0.9	57.5	45	03 19	04 00	04 32	20 07	21 00	21 49	22 43
D 13	15 28.4	18.6	183 40.5	8.1	18 22.6	0.9	57.5	N 40	03 41	04 17	04 47	19 55	20 49	21 39	22 33
A 14	30 28.3	18.9	198 07.6	8.1	18 23.5	0.7	57.5	35	03 59	04 32	04 59	19 45	20 39	21 30	22 25
Y 15	45 28.2	.. 19.2	212 34.7	8.1	18 24.2	0.6	57.5	30	04 27	04 55	05 20	19 28	20 23	21 15	22 18
16	60 28.1	19.5	227 01.8	8.0	18 24.8	0.6	57.5	20	04 48	05 15	05 38	19 13	20 08	21 02	22 06
17	75 28.0	19.8	241 28.8	8.0	18 25.4	0.4	57.6	N 10	05 06	05 32	05 55	18 59	19 54	20 50	21 55
18	90 27.9	N22 20.1	255 55.8	7.9	S18 25.8	0.3	57.6	0	05 22	05 49	06 11	18 45	19 41	20 38	21 45
19	105 27.8	20.4	270 22.7	8.0	18 26.1	0.2	57.6	S 10	05 38	06 05	06 29	18 30	19 26	20 24	21 35
20	120 27.7	20.7	284 49.7	7.9	18 26.3	0.0	57.6	20	05 53	06 23	06 49	18 13	19 10	20 09	21 24
21	135 27.6	.. 21.0	299 16.6	7.9	18 26.3	0.3	57.7	30	06 01	06 33	07 01	18 03	19 00	20 01	21 11
22	150 27.5	21.3	313 43.5	7.8	18 26.3	0.1	57.7	35	06 10	06 44	07 14	17 52	18 49	19 51	21 04
23	165 27.4	21.6	328 10.3	7.8	18 26.2	0.3	57.7	40	06 20	06 57	07 30	17 38	18 36	19 39	20 56
4 00	180 27.3	N22 21.9	342 37.1	7.9	S18 25.9	0.4	57.7	45	06 31	07 12	07 50	17 22	18 20	19 25	20 46
01	195 27.2	22.2	357 04.0	7.8	18 25.5	0.4	57.7	S 50	06 36	07 19	07 59	17 15	18 13	19 18	20 34
02	210 27.1	22.5	11 30.7	7.8	18 25.1	0.6	57.8	52	06 41	07 26	08 09	17 06	18 04	19 11	20 29
03	225 27.0	.. 22.8	25 57.5	7.8	18 24.5	0.7	57.8	54	06 46	07 35	08 21	16 57	17 55	19 02	20 23
04	240 26.9	23.1	40 24.3	7.7	18 23.8	0.8	57.8	56	06 53	07 44	08 34	16 46	17 44	18 53	20 16
05	255 26.8	23.4	54 51.0	7.7	18 23.0	0.9	57.8	S 60	06 59	07 55	08 50	16 34	17 32	18 42	20 09
06	270 26.7	N22 23.7	69 17.7	7.7	S18 22.1	1.1	57.8	Lat.	Sunset	Twilight Civil	Twilight Naut.	Moonset 3	Moonset 4	Moonset 5	Moonset 6
07	285 26.6	24.0	83 44.4	7.7	18 21.0	1.1	57.9								00 00
T 08	300 26.4	24.3	98 11.1	7.6	18 19.9	1.3	57.9								
H 09	315 26.3	.. 24.6	112 37.7	7.7	18 18.6	1.3	57.9								
U 10	330 26.2	24.9	127 04.4	7.6	18 17.3	1.5	57.9	°	h m	h m	h m	h m	h m	h m	h m
R 11	345 26.1	25.1	141 31.0	7.6	18 15.8	1.6	57.9	N 72	▭	▭	▭	■■■	■■■	02 47	05 08
S 12	0 26.0	N22 25.4	155 57.6	7.7	S18 14.2	1.7	58.0	N 70	▭	▭	▭	02 02	02 47	04 07	05 48
D 13	15 25.9	25.7	170 24.3	7.6	18 12.5	1.8	58.0	68	23 00	////	////	02 44	03 33	04 46	06 15
A 14	30 25.8	26.0	184 50.9	7.6	18 10.7	1.9	58.0	66	22 07	////	////	03 12	04 03	05 12	06 36
Y 15	45 25.7	.. 26.3	199 17.5	7.5	18 08.8	2.1	58.0	64	21 35	////	////	03 34	04 26	05 33	06 52
16	60 25.6	26.6	213 44.0	7.6	18 06.7	2.1	58.0	62	21 12	22 40	////	03 51	04 44	05 49	07 06
17	75 25.5	26.9	228 10.6	7.6	18 04.6	2.3	58.1	60	21 12	22 40	////	04 06	04 59	06 03	07 18
18	90 25.4	N22 27.2	242 37.2	7.5	S18 02.3	2.4	58.1	N 58	20 53	22 03	////	04 18	05 11	06 15	07 27
19	105 25.3	27.5	257 03.7	7.6	17 59.9	2.4	58.1	56	20 38	21 37	////	04 29	05 22	06 25	07 36
20	120 25.2	27.7	271 30.3	7.6	17 57.5	2.6	58.1	54	20 25	21 17	22 47	04 38	05 32	06 34	07 44
21	135 25.1	.. 28.0	285 56.9	7.5	17 54.9	2.7	58.1	52	20 13	21 00	22 12	04 47	05 40	06 42	07 51
22	150 25.0	28.3	300 23.4	7.6	17 52.2	2.8	58.2	50	20 03	20 46	21 48	04 54	05 48	06 49	07 57
23	165 24.9	28.6	314 50.0	7.5	17 49.4	3.0	58.2	45	19 42	20 18	21 06	05 11	06 05	07 05	08 10
5 00	180 24.7	N22 28.9	329 16.5	7.6	S17 46.4	3.0	58.2	N 40	19 25	19 57	20 38	05 24	06 18	07 18	08 21
01	195 24.6	29.2	343 43.1	7.5	17 43.4	3.2	58.2	35	19 10	19 40	20 16	05 35	06 29	07 28	08 30
02	210 24.5	29.4	358 09.6	7.6	17 40.2	3.2	58.2	30	18 58	19 25	19 58	05 45	06 39	07 38	08 39
03	225 24.4	.. 29.7	12 36.2	7.5	17 37.0	3.4	58.2	20	18 37	19 01	19 30	06 02	06 57	07 54	08 53
04	240 24.3	30.0	27 02.7	7.5	17 33.6	3.4	58.3	N 10	18 19	18 42	19 08	06 17	07 11	08 08	09 05
05	255 24.2	30.3	41 29.3	7.5	17 30.2	3.6	58.3	0	18 02	18 24	18 50	06 31	07 25	08 21	09 16
06	270 24.1	N22 30.6	55 55.8	7.6	S17 26.6	3.7	58.3	S 10	17 45	18 08	18 34	06 44	07 39	08 34	09 28
07	285 24.0	30.8	70 22.4	7.6	17 22.9	3.8	58.3	20	17 28	17 51	18 19	06 59	07 54	08 48	09 40
08	300 23.9	31.1	84 49.0	7.5	17 19.1	3.9	58.3	30	17 07	17 34	18 03	07 16	08 11	09 04	09 53
F 09	315 23.8	.. 31.4	99 15.5	7.6	17 15.2	4.0	58.3	35	16 56	17 24	17 55	07 26	08 21	09 13	10 01
R 10	330 23.7	31.7	113 42.1	7.6	17 11.2	4.2	58.4	40	16 42	17 12	17 46	07 37	08 32	09 23	10 10
I 11	345 23.6	32.0	128 08.7	7.6	17 07.0	4.2	58.4	45	16 26	17 00	17 36	07 50	08 45	09 36	10 21
D 12	0 23.4	N22 32.2	142 35.3	7.6	S17 02.8	4.3	58.4	S 50	16 07	16 45	17 26	08 06	09 01	09 50	10 33
A 13	15 23.3	32.5	157 01.9	7.7	16 58.5	4.5	58.4	52	15 57	16 38	17 21	08 14	09 09	09 57	10 39
Y 14	30 23.2	32.8	171 28.6	7.6	16 54.0	4.5	58.4	54	15 47	16 30	17 15	08 22	09 17	10 05	10 45
15	45 23.1	.. 33.1	185 55.2	7.6	16 49.5	4.7	58.4	56	15 35	16 21	17 10	08 32	09 27	10 14	10 53
16	60 23.0	33.3	200 21.8	7.7	16 44.8	4.8	58.5	58	15 22	16 12	17 04	08 43	09 37	10 23	11 01
17	75 22.9	33.6	214 48.5	7.7	16 40.0	4.8	58.5	S 60	15 06	16 01	16 57	08 55	09 50	10 34	11 10
18	90 22.8	N22 33.9	229 15.2	7.7	S16 35.2	5.0	58.5		SUN			MOON			
19	105 22.7	34.1	243 41.9	7.7	16 30.2	5.1	58.5								
20	120 22.6	34.4	258 08.6	7.7	16 25.1	5.1	58.5	Day	Eqn. of Time 00ʰ	Eqn. of Time 12ʰ	Mer. Pass.	Mer. Pass. Upper	Mer. Pass. Lower	Age	Phase
21	135 22.5	.. 34.7	272 35.3	7.7	16 20.0	5.3	58.5	d	m s	m s	h m	h m	h m	d	%
22	150 22.3	34.9	287 02.0	7.7	16 14.7	5.4	58.6	3	01 59	01 54	11 58	00 18	12 45	16	99
23	165 22.2	35.2	301 28.7	7.8	S16 09.3	5.5	58.6	4	01 49	01 44	11 58	01 12	13 40	17	96
	SD 15.8	d 0.3	SD 15.7		15.8		15.9	5	01 39	01 34	11 58	02 08	14 35	18	91

we add the .3 to the declination given at 1300 hours, so we have the following:

GHA at 13 hours 15°23.3'
+ Increments and Corrections   14°02.5'
                                    GHA 29°25.8'

_____

29°25.8' and that is the GHA at the time of sight

The declination at 1300 hours is N 22°32.5' plus .3' gives us a declination time at the observation of N 22°32.8'.

That wasn't too difficult, was it? And this, my friends, is the standard procedure for all sun sights. Find the GHA and declination at the exact time of the sight. We will go over this again, so don't fret. Work slowly and try to understand why we are doing what we are.

So now we have the GHA and the declination. In order to use the HO249 tables we need specific entering arguments that will allow us to use these tables. These arguments are local hour angle, declination, and latitude. All of them are to be entered in whole numbers of degrees with no minutes and no tenths.

The LHA we will find from the GHA and the latitude is actually an assumed latitude based on our DR. In this case, the DR latitude is 40°25' N, so we will use an assumed latitude of 40°. If our DR was 40°40' N, we would use an assumed latitude of 41° because 40°40' N is closer to 41° than it is to 40°.

Okay. So now we need to find LHA. But how do we find it? Earlier, I mentioned the concept of Assumed Position in the use of the tables. To recapitulate, the tables cannot possibly have every position tabulated. So we tabulate for the whole number of degrees with no minutes or tenths as a means of entering the tables. We create an Assumed Position based on our own dead reckoning position that allows us to use the tables. In short, if from an Assumed Position we get an Hc of X degrees (which is in the tables), we compare our actual Ho to the Hc calculated from an Assumed Position and we calculate our actual position in relation to the Assumed Position by comparing the Ho to the Hc measuring that in miles. This is called the intercept. Sound confusing? You betcha. But don't get bogged down. We will go over it again.

All LHA has to be in whole numbers to use HO249 and HO229 as well. Therefore, we create an assumed longitude based on our dead reckoning longitude, so that when subtracted it from the GHA in west longitude we get an LHA of a whole number. This allows us to use the tables. Let's look at an example.

GHA	29°25.8'	DEC. N 22°32.8
-Ass. Long	68°25.8'	
	———	
		Ass. Latitude 40°
GHA	29°25.8'	
+	360°	
	389°25.8'	
Ass. Long.	68°25.8'	
LHA	321°	

More on Sight Reduction

We'll now focus on the reduction of the sextant observation (referred to as the Hs) to the observed sextant altitude (Ho). Ho is what we are always seeking and is derived directly from the sextant observation of the sun. To put it another way, the Hs is like unrefined gold when it is mined. It has to undergo a process of reduction before the pure gold is extracted. So when we reduce a sextant sight, we are correcting our sextant sight so that it becomes suitable for use. Every observation taken must be reduced before it has any value. Every time we take a sextant observation we will go through the process we are about to discuss. Hs always needs to be reduced to Ho.

Let's say that at X hours we take an observation of the sun. Most navigators like to use the lower limb, as it seems easier to shoot with, but the upper limb—or edge—can be used as well. As a matter of course, it's not a bad practice to familiarize yourself with both. There will be times when the lower limb of the sun is obscured by clouds—or vice versa, mathematically, what we are actually aiming for is not the edge or the limb of the sun but the exact center. Of course, there is no mark for that on the celestial body, so we have to factor in by either adding or subtracting corrections to get to the mathematical center of the sun, depending on which limb—either upper or lower—we have observed.

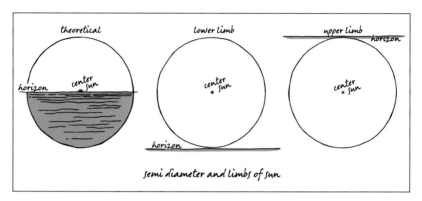

Semi-Diameter and Limbs of the Sun.

Let's do an example.

Go to the daily sun pages for March 17 (page 81) and notice that at the bottom of the page are the letters SD in bold. The number on this day is 16.1. The SD refers to the semi-diameter of the sun. In other words, at some times the earth is closer to the sun and at other times further away. Interestingly enough, the earth is closer to the sun and the SD has a larger value during the winter months and further away during the summer. At first that appears counterintuitive because it would make sense for the earth to be closer to the sun during our summer months when it is hot. But remember, it is not the distance from the sun that causes the seasons to change but the axis of the earth tilting toward or away from the sun. (Note that we are referring to the Northern Hemisphere.) During the summer months, the tilt of the earth favors the Northern Hemisphere, whereas the Southern Hemisphere is tilted away from the sun; vice versa is true during the winter. In reality, the diameter of the sun is about 32', so when the SD number refers to the angular distance from a limb to the center in the case of March 17 that is 16.1'. In June it is 15.8'. This number is part of the third correction in our sight reduction—a semi-diameter correction will be applied when reducing a sight.

March

June

2015 MARCH 17, 18, 19 (TUES., WED., THURS.)

©Copyright United Kingdom Hydrographic Office 2014

2015 JUNE 6, 7, 8 (SAT., SUN., MON.)   115

©Copyright United Kingdom Hydrographic Office 2014

DIP Table

DIP

Ht. of Eye (m)	Corrⁿ	Ht. of Eye (ft)	Ht. of Eye (m/ft)	Corrⁿ
m	′	ft.	m	′
2·4	−2·8	8·0	1·0 − 1·8	
2·6	−2·9	8·6	1·5 − 2·2	
2·8	−2·9	9·2	2·0 − 2·5	
3·0	−3·0	9·8	2·5 − 2·8	
3·2	−3·1	10·5	3·0 − 3·0	
3·4	−3·2	11·2		
3·6	−3·3	11·9	See table ←	
3·8	−3·4	12·6		
4·0	−3·5	13·3	m	′
4·3	−3·6	14·1	20 − 7·9	
4·5	−3·7	14·9	22 − 8·3	
4·7	−3·8	15·7	24 − 8·6	
5·0	−3·9	16·5	26 − 9·0	
5·2	−4·0	17·4	28 − 9·3	
5·5	−4·1	18·3		
5·8	−4·2	19·1	30 − 9·6	
6·1	−4·3	20·1	32 − 10·0	
6·3	−4·4	21·0	34 − 10·3	
6·6	−4·5	22·0	36 − 10·6	
6·9	−4·6	22·9	38 − 10·8	
7·2	−4·7	23·9		
7·5	−4·8	24·9	40 − 11·1	
7·9	−4·9	26·0	42 − 11·4	
8·2	−5·0	27·1	44 − 11·7	
8·5	−5·1	28·1	46 − 11·9	
8·8	−5·2	29·2	48 − 12·2	
9·2	−5·3	30·4	ft.	′
9·5	−5·4	31·5	2 − 1·4	
9·9	−5·5	32·7	4 − 1·9	
10·3	−5·6	33·9	6 − 2·4	
10·6	−5·7	35·1	8 − 2·7	
11·0	−5·8	36·3	10 − 3·1	
11·4	−5·9	37·6		
11·8	−6·0	38·9	See table ←	
12·2	−6·1	40·1	ft.	′
12·6	−6·2	41·5	70 − 8·1	
13·0	−6·3	42·8	75 − 8·4	
13·4	−6·4	44·2	80 − 8·7	
13·8	−6·5	45·5	85 − 8·9	
14·2	−6·6	46·9	90 − 9·2	
14·7	−6·7	48·4	95 − 9·5	
15·1	−6·8	49·8		
15·5	−6·9	51·3	100 − 9·7	
16·0	−7·0	52·8	105 − 9·9	
16·5	−7·1	54·3	110 − 10·2	
16·9	−7·2	55·8	115 − 10·4	
17·4	−7·3	57·4	120 − 10·6	
17·9	−7·4	58·9	125 − 10·8	
18·4	−7·5	60·5		
18·8	−7·6	62·1	130 − 11·1	
19·3	−7·7	63·8	135 − 11·3	
19·8	−7·8	65·4	140 − 11·5	
20·4	−7·9	67·1	145 − 11·7	
20·9	−8·0	68·8	150 − 11·9	
21·4	−8·1	70·5	155 − 12·1	

Before delving further, remember the mathematical conceit here is that we are actually at the center of the earth and observing the center of the sun. Given the fact that we are on the surface of the earth, we have to mathematically manipulate the numbers to make it appear as if we are in the center. We must do the following to reduce it accurately: We need to know our height of eye above the horizon, if there is an Index Error in the tool itself, the month we take our sight, and whether we are observing an upper or lower limb (edge) of the sun. First let's look at height of eye. Obviously, we want to reduce the height of eye so that we can compensate for the difference in the height of the observer above sea level. The higher we are above the horizon, the greater correction that we have to include. We want to mathematically reduce our height of eye to sea level. This is referred to as the dip, and it is always subtracted, as it must be, because unless swimming or on a life raft, you will always be above the horizon. So how do we find out what the height of eye is? Usually on a sailboat, calculate a dip correction of 9 or 10 feet. That means that I can safely assume that that is my height above sea level when taking an observation. It may be a little bit more or a little less than that, but the difference between 8 feet and 12 feet is not so great. If you are on an airplane, obviously, the dip correction will be much greater, but I will assume that most of the readers are sailing not flying.

The dip table and all other corrections necessary for the correction of Hs to Ho (sextant altitude to observed altitude) can be found inside the front cover of the *Nautical Almanac* and is labelled as "Altitudes Correction Table 10°-90° Sun, Stars, Planets."

LAT 15°

Hc	Z		Hc	Z		Hc	Z		Hc	Z		Hc	Z		Hc	Z		Hc	Z		Hc	Z		Hc	Z		Hc	Z		Hc	Z		Hc	Z		Hc	Z		Hc	Z		Hc	Z	LHA

(Full 15-column celestial navigation sight-reduction table for Latitude 15°, declinations 0° through 14°, with columns for altitude Hc and azimuth Z at each degree of declination.)

LAT 14°

LHA
291
292
293
294
295
296
297
298
299
300
301
302
303
304
305
306
307
308
309
310
311
312
313
314
315
316
317
318
319
320
321
322
323
324
325
326
327
328
329
330
331
332
333
334
335
336
337
338
339
340
341
342
343
344
345
346
347
348
349
350
351
352
353
354
355
356
357
358
359
360

LAT 14°

Column headers across the table: Hc d Z (repeated for each degree of latitude)

Degree columns: 15° 16° 17° 18° 19° 20° 21° 22° 23° 24° 25° 26° 27° 28° 29°

DECLINATION (15°–29°) CONTRARY NAME TO LATITUDE

The *Sight Reduction Tables for Air Navigation* (HO249) is my preferred tabular method. They are cumbersome and confusing at first to use, but a bit of practice will be of great value. They come in three volumes, but only Volumes II and III will be of interest here. Volume I is for Selected Stars, which is not pertinent for our purposes. Volume II covers latitudes 0° to 40° with declinations from 0° to 29°. Volume III covers latitudes from 39° to 89°, again with declinations from 0° to 29°. These volumes are good forever, so you only have to buy them once. They are perfect for observations of the sun as the declination of the sun is never more than 23°5'. The included latitudes are for both north and south. (See previous two pages.)

The entering arguments of the sight reduction tables have very specific requirements. In order to use the tables to find our position, we need to fulfill the following:

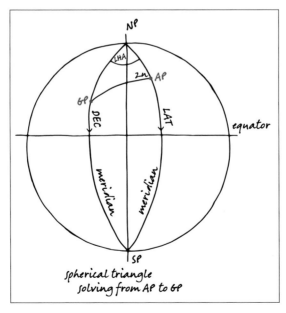

Spherical Triangle. What the Sight Reduction Tables Solve.

On pages 84 and 85 are examples of a part of the table. What we are doing in essence is comparing our calculated sextants angle (Hc) given in the tables from an Assumed Position to our actual observed sextant angle (Ho), derived from the actual latitude and longitude of where we were at the time of the observation. To put it another way, if we know the Hc of an observation based on an Assumed Position, we can then compare our Ho to that Hc; from there, we find out if we are further away or closer to the GP of the celestial object, in this case the sun. Usually the difference between the Hc and Ho is a matter of minutes of arc (nautical miles). This is the essence of the intercept method. If our Ho is larger than the Hc, then we are closer to the GP by the difference. If the Ho is less than the Hc, then we are farther away, as based on the difference between the two. This process is called the intercept method. The way to remember Ho Mo To, which means Ho is more than the Ho, and toward the GP (page 42, Intercept Diagram).

It is very easy to make mistakes when using these tables. There are various prompts and instructions all over the pages, so being alert is important here. It is important to see if you are entering the right pages. There are pages that state at the top that declination is either contrary or is the same as the latitude. This means that if you are in the northern latitudes, the declination of the sun is south of the equator—or the declination of the sun can be the same as the observer if both are in either the Northern or Southern Hemisphere. Also, the pages vary with the declination, so go to the page with the declination of the sun that applies to your observation. In Volume II, the declinations are either (15° to 29°) or (0° to 14°).

There are a lot of numbers on these pages. Don't get overwhelmed by them. Pay attention to what you are doing, which is solving the celestial triangle for an Assumed Position. Proceed slowly.

The entering arguments must be followed in order to get the tables to work for you. Three numbers are required: an assumed latitude derived from the DR latitude; LHA of a whole number of degrees; and declination. An example would be based on DR longitude.

When you have all three numbers—LHA, latitude, and declination—you can turn to the Tables. Go to the page with the correct Assumed Latitude and make certain you are on the page for the correct declination. The tops of the pages are different, with one page labeling declination from 0° to 14° and another page labeled 15° to 29°. Also it is important to notice that the top of the pages over declination read either "Same" or "Contrary." This means that if we are in the Northern Hemisphere and the sun has a south declination, then we are Contrary. If, on the other hand, both the declination of the sun and the latitude of the observer are in the same hemisphere, we go to the page labeled Same. The LHA is listed in smaller numbers on the left side of the page and at the right side of the page. When you are looking for the Hc (or calculated altitude), you place a straight edge under the LHA and look under the column labeled as "Declination." All of this sounds cumbersome but after a few attempts it will become obvious. It is important to use a straight edge when finding the LHA because it is easy to make an error at this step, especially when out at sea in a bouncy boat.

Recall that we are looking for the Hc, d, and Zn, which together gives us the calculated altitude and bearing to the sun from the Assumed Position. We then compare this Hc to our Ho and get our intercept, which we use to plot our LOP. Here it may be necessary to convert the azimuth angle of the sun (Z) to the actual bearing of the sun (Zn). The formula for this can be found at the top of every page of the tables. For example, in the morning, you take an observation of the sun and the bearing is 230°; you therefore know that cannot be possible, as before noon the sun would be bearing to the east. So then, following the printed formula, you convert the Z to Zn.

A note here about azimuth (Zn) and azimuth angle (Z). It almost seems as if the tables were designed to make things as difficult as possible for the neophyte navigator. The azimuth and azimuth angle are a good example of this. My

N. Lat. {LHA greater than 180°....... Zn=Z
{LHA less than 180°.........Zn=360-Z

DECLINATION (0°-14°) SAME NAME AS LATITUDE

LHA	Hc 0°	d	Z	Hc 1°	d	Z	Hc 2°	d	Z	Hc 3°	d	Z	Hc 4°	d	Z	Hc 5°	d	Z	Hc 6°	d	Z	Hc 7°	d	Z	Hc 8°	d	Z	Hc 9°	d	Z	Hc 10°	d	Z
0	80 00	+60	180	81 00	+60	180	82 00	+60	180	83 00	+60	180	84 00	+60	180	85 00	+60	180	86 00	+60	180	87 00	+60	180	88 00	+60	180	89 00	+60	180	90 00	-60	
1	79 57	60	174	80 57	59	174	81 56	60	173	82 56	59	172	83 55	59	171	84 54	59	169	85 53	58	166	86 51	55	162	87 46	50	154	88 36	25	135	89 01	25	90
2	79 48	59	169	80 47	58	167	81 45	58	166	82 43	58	164	83 41	56	162	84 37	56	158	85 32	52	154	86 24	49	146	87 11	36	135	87 47	15	117	88 02	14	90
3	79 34	57	163	80 31	57	162	81 28	56	159	82 24	54	157	83 18	53	153	84 11	50	149	85 01	46	143	85 47	39	135	86 26	27	124	86 53	10	108	87 03	10	90
4	79 14	56	158	80 10	54	156	81 04	53	153	81 57	51	150	82 48	49	146	83 37	45	141	84 22	40	135	85 02	32	127	85 34	22	117	85 56	8	104	86 04	7	90
5	78 50	+53	153	79 43	+52	151	80 35	+50	148	81 25	+48	144	82 13	+45	140	82 58	+40	135	83 38	+35	129	84 13	+27	121	84 40	+18	112	84 58	+7	101	85 05	-6	90
6	78 21	51	149	79 12	49	146	80 01	48	143	80 49	44	139	81 33	41	135	82 14	36	130	82 50	31	124	83 21	24	116	83 45	15	108	84 00	6	99	84 06	5	90
7	77 49	48	145	78 37	47	142	79 24	44	139	80 08	41	135	80 49	38	130	81 27	33	125	82 00	27	120	82 27	21	113	82 48	13	106	83 01	5	98	83 06	3	89
8	77 13	46	141	77 59	44	138	78 43	42	135	79 25	38	131	80 03	35	127	80 38	30	122	81 08	24	116	81 32	19	110	81 51	12	104	82 03	4	97	82 07	3	89
9	76 35	44	138	77 19	41	135	78 00	39	131	78 39	36	128	79 15	32	123	79 47	27	119	80 14	23	114	80 37	16	108	80 53	11	102	81 04	4	96	81 08	2	89
10	75 54	+41	135	76 35	+40	132	77 15	+36	128	77 51	+33	125	78 24	+30	121	78 54	+25	116	79 19	+21	111	79 40	+15	106	79 55	+10	101	80 05	+4	95	80 09	-2	89
11	75 11	39	132	75 50	37	129	76 27	35	126	77 02	31	122	77 33	27	118	78 00	24	114	78 24	19	109	78 43	14	105	78 57	9	100	79 06	4	94	79 10	2	89
12	74 26	37	129	75 03	36	126	75 39	32	123	76 11	29	120	76 40	26	116	77 06	22	112	77 28	18	108	77 46	13	103	77 59	8	99	78 07	4	94	78 11	1	89
13	73 39	36	127	74 15	33	124	74 48	31	121	75 19	28	118	75 47	24	114	76 11	20	110	76 31	17	106	76 48	12	102	77 00	8	98	77 08	4	93	77 12	1	89
14	72 51	34	125	73 25	32	122	73 57	29	119	74 26	26	116	74 52	23	112	75 15	20	109	75 35	15	105	75 50	12	101	76 02	7	97	76 09	4	93	76 13	0	89
15	72 02	+33	123	72 35	+30	120	73 05	+28	117	73 33	+24	114	73 57	+22	111	74 19	+18	108	74 37	+15	104	74 52	+11	100	75 03	+7	97	75 10	+4	93	75 14	-1	89
16	71 12	31	121	71 43	29	119	72 12	26	116	72 38	24	113	73 02	20	110	73 22	18	106	73 40	14	103	73 54	10	100	74 04	7	96	74 11	4	92	74 15	1	89
17	70 21	30	120	70 51	28	117	71 19	25	114	71 44	22	111	72 06	20	108	72 26	16	105	72 42	14	102	72 56	10	99	73 06	6	95	73 12	4	92	73 16	-1	89
18	69 29	29	118	69 58	26	116	70 24	24	113	70 48	22	110	71 10	18	107	71 28	16	104	71 44	13	101	71 57	10	98	72 07	6	95	72 13	4	92	72 17	0	88
19	68 37	27	117	69 04	26	114	69 30	23	112	69 53	20	109	70 13	18	106	70 31	15	104	70 46	13	101	70 59	9	98	71 08	6	95	71 14	4	91	71 18	0	88
20	67 44	+26	116	68 10	+25	113	68 35	+22	111	68 57	+19	108	69 16	+18	105	69 34	+14	103	69 48	+12	100	70 00	+9	97	70 09	+6	94	70 15	+3	91	70 18	+1	88
21	66 50	26	114	67 16	23	112	67 39	21	110	68 00	19	107	68 19	17	105	68 36	14	102	68 50	11	99	69 01	9	97	69 10	6	94	69 16	3	91	69 19	1	88
22	65 56	25	113	66 21	22	111	66 43	21	109	67 04	18	106	67 22	16	104	67 38	13	101	67 51	12	99	68 03	8	96	68 11	6	94	68 17	3	91	68 20	1	88
23	65 02	24	112	65 26	21	110	65 47	20	108	66 07	18	106	66 25	15	103	66 40	13	101	66 53	11	98	67 04	8	96	67 12	6	93	67 18	3	91	67 21	1	88
24	64 07	23	111	64 30	21	109	64 51	19	107	65 10	17	105	65 27	15	102	65 42	13	100	65 55	10	98	66 05	8	95	66 13	6	93	66 19	3	90	66 22	1	88
25	63 12	+22	110	63 34	+20	108	63 54	+19	106	64 13	+16	104	64 29	+15	102	64 44	+12	100	64 56	+10	97	65 06	+8	95	65 14	+6	93	65 20	+3	90	65 23	+1	88
26	62 16	22	110	62 38	19	108	62 57	18	106	63 15	16	103	63 31	14	101	63 45	12	99	63 57	10	97	64 07	8	95	64 15	6	92	64 21	3	90	64 24	1	88
27	61 20	21	109	61 41	19	107	62 01	18	105	62 18	15	103	62 33	14	101	62 47	12	99	62 59	9	96	63 08	8	94	63 16	6	92	63 22	3	90	63 25	2	88
28	60 24	21	108	60 45	18	106	61 03	17	104	61 20	15	102	61 35	13	100	61 48	12	98	62 00	9	96	62 09	8	94	62 17	5	92	62 22	4	90	62 26	2	88
29	59 28	20	107	59 48	18	106	60 06	16	104	60 22	15	102	60 37	13	100	60 50	11	98	61 01	9	96	61 10	8	94	61 18	5	92	61 23	4	90	61 27	2	88
30	58 32	+19	107	58 51	+17	105	59 08	+16	103	59 24	+15	101	59 39	+12	99	59 51	+11	97	60 02	+9	95	60 11	+8	93	60 19	+5	91	60 24	+4	89	60 28	+2	87
31	57 34	19	106	57 54	17	104	58 11	15	103	58 26	13	101	58 40	13	99	58 53	10	97	59 03	9	95	59 12	8	93	59 20	5	91	59 25	4	89	59 29	2	87
32	56 38	18	106	56 56	17	104	57 13	15	102	57 28	14	100	57 42	12	98	57 54	11	97	58 05	8	95	58 13	8	93	58 21	5	91	58 26	4	89	58 30	2	87
33	55 41	18	105	55 59	16	103	56 15	15	102	56 30	13	100	56 43	12	98	56 55	11	96	57 06	8	94	57 14	8	93	57 22	5	91	57 27	4	89	57 31	2	87
34	54 44	17	104	55 01	16	103	55 17	15	101	55 32	13	99	55 45	12	98	55 57	10	96	56 07	8	94	56 15	7	92	56 22	6	91	56 28	4	89	56 32	2	87

TABLE 5.—Correction to Tabulat[ed]

d / ′	1	2	3	4	5	6	7	8	9	10	11	12	13	14	15	16	17	18	19	20	21	22	23	24	25	26	27	28	29
0	0	0	0	0	0	0	0	0	0	0	0	0	0	0	0	0	0	0	0	0	0	0	0	0	0	0	0	0	0
1	0	0	0	0	0	0	0	0	0	0	0	0	0	0	0	0	0	0	0	0	0	0	0	0	0	0	0	0	0
2	0	0	0	0	0	0	0	0	0	0	0	0	1	1	1	1	1	1	1	1	1	1	1	1	1	1	1	1	1
3	0	0	0	0	0	0	0	0	0	1	1	1	1	1	1	1	1	1	1	1	1	1	1	1	1	1	1	1	1
4	0	0	0	0	0	0	0	1	1	1	1	1	1	1	1	1	1	1	1	2	2	2	2	2	2	2	2	2	2
5	0	0	0	0	0	0	1	1	1	1	1	1	1	1	1	1	1	2	2	2	2	2	2	2	2	2	2	2	2
6	0	0	0	0	0	0	1	1	1	1	1	1	1	1	2	2	2	2	2	2	2	2	2	2	2	3	3	3	3
7	0	0	0	0	1	1	1	1	1	1	1	1	2	2	2	2	2	2	2	2	2	3	3	3	3	3	3	3	3
8	0	0	0	1	1	1	1	1	1	1	1	2	2	2	2	2	2	2	3	3	3	3	3	3	3	3	4	4	4
9	0	0	0	1	1	1	1	1	1	2	2	2	2	2	2	2	3	3	3	3	3	3	3	4	4	4	4	4	4
10	0	0	0	1	1	1	1	1	2	2	2	2	2	3	3	3	3	3	3	3	4	4	4	4	4	4	4	5	5
11	0	0	1	1	1	1	1	1	2	2	2	2	2	3	3	3	4	4	4	4	4	5	5	5	5	5	5	5	5
12	0	0	1	1	1	1	1	2	2	2	2	2	3	3	3	3	3	4	4	4	4	4	5	5	5	5	5	6	6
13	0	0	1	1	1	1	2	2	2	2	2	3	3	3	3	3	4	4	4	4	5	5	5	5	5	6	6	6	6
14	0	0	1	1	1	1	2	2	2	2	3	3	3	3	4	4	4	4	4	5	5	5	5	6	6	6	6	7	7
15	0	0	1	1	1	2	2	2	2	2	3	3	3	4	4	4	4	4	5	5	5	6	6	6	6	6	7	7	7
16	0	1	1	1	1	2	2	2	2	3	3	3	3	4	4	4	5	5	5	5	6	6	6	6	7	7	7	7	8
17	0	1	1	1	1	2	2	2	3	3	3	3	4	4	4	5	5	5	5	6	6	6	7	7	7	7	8	8	8
18	0	1	1	1	2	2	2	2	3	3	3	4	4	4	4	5	5	5	6	6	6	7	7	7	8	8	8	8	9
19	0	1	1	1	2	2	2	3	3	3	3	4	4	4	5	5	5	6	6	6	7	7	7	8	8	8	9	9	9
20	0	1	1	1	2	2	2	3	3	3	4	4	4	5	5	5	6	6	6	7	7	7	8	8	8	9	9	9	10
21	0	1	1	1	2	2	2	3	3	4	4	4	5	5	5	6	6	6	7	7	7	8	8	8	9	9	9	10	10
22	0	1	1	1	2	2	3	3	3	4	4	4	5	5	6	6	6	7	7	7	8	8	8	9	9	10	10	10	11
23	0	1	1	2	2	2	3	3	3	4	4	5	5	5	6	6	7	7	7	8	8	8	9	9	10	10	10	11	11
24	0	1	1	2	2	2	3	3	4	4	4	5	5	6	6	6	7	7	8	8	8	9	9	10	10	10	11	11	12
25	0	1	1	2	2	2	3	3	4	4	5	5	5	6	6	7	7	8	8	8	9	9	10	10	10	11	11	12	12
26	0	1	1	2	2	3	3	3	4	4	5	5	6	6	6	7	7	8	8	9	9	10	10	10	11	11	12	12	13
27	0	1	1	2	2	3	3	4	4	5	5	5	6	6	7	7	8	8	9	9	10	10	11	11	12	12	13	13	13
28	0	1	1	2	2	3	3	4	4	5	5	6	6	7	7	7	8	8	9	9	10	10	11	11	12	12	13	13	14
29	0	1	1	2	2	3	3	4	4	5	5	6	6	7	7	8	8	9	9	10	10	11	11	12	12	13	13	14	14
30	0	1	2	2	2	3	4	4	4	5	6	6	6	7	8	8	8	9	10	10	10	11	12	12	12	13	14	14	14
31	1	1	2	2	3	3	4	4	5	5	6	6	7	7	8	8	9	9	10	10	11	11	12	12	13	13	14	14	15
32	1	1	2	2	3	3	4	4	5	5	6	6	7	7	8	9	9	10	10	11	11	12	12	13	13	14	14	15	15
33	1	1	2	2	3	3	4	4	5	6	6	7	7	8	8	9	9	10	10	11	12	12	13	13	14	14	15	15	16
34	1	1	2	2	3	3	4	5	5	6	6	7	7	8	8	9	10	10	11	11	12	12	13	14	14	15	15	16	16
35	1	1	2	2	3	4	4	5	5	6	6	7	8	8	9	9	10	10	11	12	12	13	13	14	15	15	16	16	17
36	1	1	2	2	3	4	4	5	5	6	7	7	8	8	9	10	10	11	12	12	13	13	14	15	15	16	16	17	17
37	1	1	2	2	3	4	4	5	6	6	7	7	8	9	9	10	10	11	12	12	13	14	14	15	15	16	17	17	18
38	1	1	2	3	3	4	4	5	6	6	7	8	8	9	10	10	11	11	12	13	13	14	15	15	16	16	17	18	18
39	1	1	2	3	3	4	5	5	6	6	7	8	8	9	10	10	11	12	12	13	14	14	15	16	17	17	18	18	19
40	1	1	2	3	3	4	5	5	6	7	7	8	9	9	10	11	11	12	13	13	14	15	15	16	17	17	18	19	19
41	1	1	2	3	3	4	5	5	6	7	8	8	9	10	10	11	12	12	13	14	14	15	16	16	17	18	18	19	20
42	1	1	2	3	4	4	5	6	6	7	8	8	9	10	10	11	12	13	13	14	15	15	16	17	18	18	19	20	20
43	1	1	2	3	4	4	5	6	6	7	8	9	10	10	11	11	12	13	14	14	15	16	16	17	18	19	19	20	21
44	1	1	2	3	4	4	5	6	7	7	8	9	10	10	11	12	12	13	14	15	15	16	17	18	18	19	20	21	21
45	1	2	2	3	4	4	5	6	7	8	8	9	10	10	11	12	13	14	14	15	16	16	17	18	19	20	20	21	22
46	1	2	2	3	4	5	5	6	7	8	8	9	10	11	12	12	13	14	15	15	16	17	18	18	19	20	21	21	22
47	1	2	2	3	4	5	5	6	7	8	9	9	10	11	12	13	13	14	15	16	16	17	18	19	20	20	21	22	23
48	1	2	2	3	4	5	6	6	7	8	9	10	10	11	12	13	14	14	15	16	17	18	18	19	20	21	22	22	23
49	1	2	2	3	4	5	6	7	7	8	9	10	11	11	12	13	14	15	16	16	17	18	19	20	20	21	22	23	24
50	1	2	2	3	4	5	6	7	8	8	9	10	11	12	12	13	14	15	16	17	18	18	19	20	21	22	22	23	24
51	1	2	3	3	4	5	6	7	8	8	9	10	11	12	13	14	14	15	16	17	18	19	20	20	21	22	23	24	25
52	1	2	3	3	4	5	6	7	8	9	10	10	11	12	13	14	15	16	16	17	18	19	20	21	22	23	23	24	25
53	1	2	3	4	4	5	6	7	8	9	10	11	11	12	13	14	15	16	17	18	19	19	20	21	22	23	24	25	26
54	1	2	3	4	4	5	6	7	8	9	10	11	12	13	14	14	15	16	17	18	19	20	21	22	(22)	23	24	25	26
55	1	2	3	4	5	6	6	7	8	9	10	11	12	13	14	15	16	16	17	18	19	20	21	22	23	24	25	26	27
56	1	2	3	4	5	6	7	7	8	9	10	11	12	13	14	15	16	17	18	19	20	21	21	22	23	24	25	26	27
57	1	2	3	4	5	6	7	8	9	10	10	11	12	13	14	15	16	17	18	19	20	21	22	23	24	25	26	27	28
58	1	2	3	4	5	6	7	8	9	10	11	12	13	14	14	15	16	17	18	19	20	21	22	23	24	25	26	27	28
59	1	2	3	4	5	6	7	8	9	10	11	12	13	14	15	16	17	18	19	20	21	22	23	24	25	26	27	28	29

ltitude for Minutes of Declination

32	33	34	35	36	37	38	39	40	41	42	43	44	45	46	47	48	49	50	51	52	53	54	55	56	57	58	59	60	d/'
0	0	0	0	0	0	0	0	0	0	0	0	0	0	0	0	0	0	0	0	0	0	0	0	0	0	0	0	0	0
1	1	1	1	1	1	1	1	1	1	1	1	1	1	1	1	1	1	1	1	1	1	1	1	1	1	1	1	1	1
1	1	1	1	1	1	1	1	1	1	1	1	1	2	2	2	2	2	2	2	2	2	2	2	2	2	2	2	2	2
2	2	2	2	2	2	2	2	2	2	2	2	2	2	2	2	2	2	3	3	3	3	3	3	3	3	3	3	3	3
2	2	2	2	2	2	3	3	3	3	3	3	3	3	3	3	3	3	3	3	3	4	4	4	4	4	4	4	4	4
3	3	3	3	3	3	3	3	3	3	4	4	4	4	4	4	4	4	4	4	4	4	4	5	5	5	5	5	5	5
3	3	3	4	4	3	4	4	4	4	4	4	4	4	4	5	5	5	5	5	5	5	5	6	6	6	6	6	6	6
4	4	4	4	4	4	4	4	4	5	5	5	5	5	5	5	6	6	6	6	6	6	6	6	7	7	7	7	7	7
4	4	4	4	4	4	4	5	5	5	5	5	5	6	6	6	6	7	7	7	7	7	7	7	7	8	8	8	8	8
5	5	5	5	5	5	5	5	5	5	6	6	6	6	6	6	6	7	7	8	8	8	8	8	8	9	9	9	9	9
5	6	6	6	6	6	6	7	7	7	7	7	7	8	8	8	8	8	8	9	9	9	9	9	10	10	10	10	10	10
6	6	6	6	7	7	7	7	7	8	8	8	8	8	8	9	9	9	9	9	10	10	10	10	11	11	11	11	11	11
6	7	7	7	7	7	8	8	8	8	9	9	9	9	9	9	10	10	10	10	10	11	11	11	11	11	12	12	12	12
7	7	7	8	8	8	8	9	9	9	9	9	10	10	10	10	10	11	11	11	11	11	12	12	12	12	13	13	13	13
7	8	8	8	8	9	9	9	9	10	10	10	10	11	11	11	11	11	12	12	12	12	12	13	13	13	14	14	14	14
8	8	8	9	9	9	10	10	10	10	10	11	11	11	12	12	12	12	13	13	13	14	14	14	14	15	15	15	15	15
9	9	9	9	10	10	10	10	11	11	11	11	12	12	12	13	13	13	13	14	14	14	14	15	15	15	15	16	16	16
9	9	10	10	10	10	11	11	11	12	12	12	13	13	13	13	14	14	14	15	15	15	16	16	16	16	16	17	17	17
10	10	10	10	11	11	11	12	12	12	13	13	13	14	14	14	15	15	15	16	16	16	16	16	17	17	17	18	18	18
10	10	11	11	11	11	12	12	12	13	13	14	14	14	15	15	15	16	16	16	16	17	17	17	18	18	18	19	19	19
11	11	11	12	12	12	13	13	13	14	14	14	15	15	15	16	16	16	17	17	17	18	18	18	19	19	19	20	20	20
11	12	12	12	13	13	13	14	14	14	15	15	15	16	16	16	17	17	18	18	18	19	19	19	20	20	20	21	21	21
12	12	12	13	13	14	14	14	15	15	15	16	16	16	17	17	18	18	18	19	19	19	20	20	21	21	21	22	22	22
12	13	13	13	14	14	15	15	15	16	16	16	17	17	17	18	18	19	19	20	20	20	21	21	21	22	22	23	23	23
13	13	14	14	14	15	15	16	16	16	17	17	18	18	18	19	19	20	20	20	21	21	22	22	22	23	23	24	24	24
13	14	14	15	15	15	16	16	17	17	18	18	18	19	19	20	20	20	21	21	22	22	22	23	23	24	24	25	25	25
14	14	15	15	16	16	16	17	17	18	18	19	19	20	20	20	21	21	22	22	23	23	23	24	24	25	25	26	26	26
14	15	15	15	16	17	17	18	18	19	19	19	20	20	21	21	22	22	22	23	23	24	24	25	25	26	26	27	27	27
15	15	16	16	17	17	18	18	19	19	20	20	21	21	21	22	22	23	23	24	24	25	25	26	26	27	27	28	28	28
15	16	16	17	17	18	18	19	19	20	20	21	21	22	22	23	23	24	24	25	25	26	26	26	27	27	28	29	29	29
16	16	17	18	18	18	19	20	20	20	21	21	22	22	23	24	24	24	25	26	26	26	27	27	28	28	29	30	30	30
17	17	18	18	19	19	20	20	20	21	22	22	23	23	24	24	25	25	26	27	27	27	28	28	29	29	30	30	31	31
17	18	18	19	19	20	20	21	21	22	22	23	23	24	25	25	26	26	27	27	28	28	29	29	30	30	31	31	32	32
18	18	19	19	20	20	21	21	22	22	23	24	24	25	25	26	26	27	27	28	29	29	30	30	31	31	32	32	33	33
18	19	19	20	20	21	21	22	23	23	24	24	25	26	26	27	27	28	28	29	29	30	31	31	32	32	33	33	34	34
19	19	20	20	21	22	22	23	23	24	25	25	26	26	27	28	28	29	29	30	31	32	32	33	34	34	34	35	35	35
19	20	20	21	22	22	23	23	24	24	25	26	26	27	27	28	29	30	30	31	31	32	33	34	34	35	35	36	36	36
20	20	21	22	22	23	23	24	25	25	26	27	27	28	28	29	30	30	31	31	32	33	33	34	35	35	36	36	37	37
20	21	22	22	23	23	24	25	25	26	27	27	28	28	29	30	30	31	32	32	33	34	34	35	35	36	37	37	38	38
21	21	22	23	23	24	25	25	26	27	27	28	29	29	30	31	31	32	32	33	34	34	35	36	36	37	38	38	39	39
21	22	23	23	24	25	25	26	27	27	28	29	29	30	31	31	32	33	33	34	35	35	36	37	37	38	39	39	40	40
22	23	23	24	25	25	26	27	27	28	29	29	30	31	31	32	33	33	34	35	36	36	37	38	38	39	40	40	41	41
22	23	24	24	25	26	27	27	28	29	29	30	31	32	32	33	34	34	35	36	36	37	38	38	39	40	41	41	42	42
23	24	24	25	26	27	27	28	29	30	31	31	32	32	33	34	35	35	36	37	37	38	39	39	40	41	42	42	43	43
23	24	25	25	26	27	28	29	29	30	31	32	32	33	34	35	35	36	37	37	38	39	40	40	41	42	42	43	44	44
24	25	26	26	27	28	28	29	30	31	32	32	33	34	34	35	36	37	38	38	39	40	40	41	42	43	44	44	45	45
25	25	26	27	28	28	29	30	31	31	32	33	34	34	35	36	37	38	38	39	40	41	41	42	43	44	44	45	46	46
25	26	27	27	28	29	30	30	31	32	33	34	34	35	36	37	38	38	39	40	41	42	43	43	44	45	45	46	47	47
26	26	27	28	29	30	30	31	32	33	33	34	35	36	37	38	38	39	40	41	42	43	43	44	45	46	46	47	48	48
26	27	28	29	29	30	31	32	33	33	34	35	36	37	38	38	39	40	41	42	42	43	44	45	46	47	47	48	49	49
27	28	28	29	30	31	32	32	33	34	35	36	37	38	38	39	40	41	42	42	43	44	45	46	47	48	48	49	50	50
27	28	29	30	31	31	32	33	34	35	36	37	37	38	39	40	41	42	42	43	44	45	46	47	48	48	49	50	51	51
28	29	29	30	31	32	33	34	34	35	36	37	38	39	40	40	41	42	43	44	45	45	46	47	48	49	50	50	51	52
28	29	30	31	32	33	33	34	35	36	37	38	39	40	40	41	42	43	44	45	46	46	47	48	49	50	51	52	52	53
29	30	31	32	32	33	34	35	36	37	38	39	40	40	41	42	43	44	45	46	47	47	48	49	50	51	52	53	53	54
29	30	31	32	33	34	35	36	37	38	38	39	40	41	42	43	44	45	46	47	48	49	50	50	51	52	53	54	55	55
30	31	32	33	34	35	35	36	37	38	39	40	41	42	43	44	45	46	47	48	49	50	51	51	52	53	54	55	56	56
30	31	32	33	34	35	36	37	38	39	40	41	42	43	44	45	46	47	48	48	50	51	52	53	54	55	55	56	57	57
31	32	33	34	35	36	37	38	39	40	41	42	43	44	44	45	46	47	48	49	50	51	52	53	54	55	56	57	58	58
31	32	33	34	35	36	37	38	39	40	41	42	43	44	45	46	47	48	49	50	51	52	53	54	55	56	57	58	59	59

advice is to follow the instructions on the top left and the bottom left of the HO249.

On the top of the page, it states that in N latitude, if LHA is greater than 180°, then Zn = Z, but if LHA is less than 180°, then Zn = 360 − 7. This means the azimuth (Zn) is actually the true bearing, measured in a clockwise direction from the observer's position to the sun. Let's explain further with the following:

Azimuth angle (Z) differs from azimuth (Zn) as it is a relative bearing measured either in a clockwise or counter-clockwise manner from 0 to 180°. It is measured relative to true north in the Northern Hemisphere and relative to true south in Southern Hemisphere. When solving for Z, you have to convert Z to Zn; don't worry, the rules for doing this are stated on every page of HO249. It is necessary to do this so we get a true bearing to the GP of the sun and not a relative one. Ponder this and follow the directions on top and bottom of the page. Don't get sidetracked or hoodwinked.

Now you have the Hc and the Zn. But up with the small letter d? What do you do with that? Recall that you entered the tables with a whole number of degrees of declination. But there are also minutes of declination that you recorded

	0°			1°			2°		
	Hc	d	Z	Hc	d	Z	Hc	d	Z
4	74 29	58	165	73 31	58	166	72 33	59	167
3	74 43	59	169	73 44	59	169	72 45	60	170
2	74 52	59	172	73 53	60	173	72 53	59	173
1	74 58	60	176	73 58	60	176	72 58	60	177
0	75 00	−60	180	74 00	−60	180	73 00	−60	180

S. Lat. { LHA greater than 180°........ Zn=180−Z
         { LHA less than 180°...........Zn=180+Z

N. Lat. { LHA greater than 180°........ Zn=Z
         { LHA less than 180°...........Zn=360−Z

	0°			1°			2°		
LHA	Hc	d	Z	Hc	d	Z	Hc	d	Z
69	20 15	17	96	19 58	17	97	19 41	17	98
68	21 13	17	96	20 56	17	97	20 39	18	98
67	22 10	16	96	21 54	18	97	21 36	18	98
66	23 08	17	97	22 51	18	98	22 33	17	99
65	24 06	−18	97	23 48	−17	98	23 31	−18	96

for the time of the sight. What to do with them? Now, you need to find the declination (latitude) of the sun at the time we took our observation. This means declination in degrees and minutes. So how do you calculate the complete declination? The tables do that all for you. At the rear of HO249 is Table 5 labeled as "Correction to Tabulated Altitude for Minutes of Declination" (pages 90-91). The table is entered with the d correction and the minutes of declination. The minutes of declination can be entered at the top and with the d correction on the side, or vice versa. The result will be the same. Let's look at an example.

Let's say we take an observation in the afternoon at a DR position that yields an Assumed Position of N 36° latitude and an LHA of 29°. The declination at the time of our sight is S 16°25.4'. The Ho of our sight is 30°48'. We have enough information to enter the sight reduction tables. We are in northernly latitude and our declination is southernly, so we enter the contrary page for latitude 36°.

Under 16° declination and at LHA 29° we see Hc 31°13'   d 54'   Z 147°

We need to find the correction for the 25' of declination so we go to Table 5 (pages 90-91) and find the d corr of 54' corresponding to the 25' of declination. This number is 22', which means we subtract those 22' from the Hc in order to find the exact Hc from our assumed position. Now do we add or subtract that number? By inspection of the d column we see a minus sign and this tells us that we subtract 22' from the Hc:

Hc   31°13'
Table 5 –   22'
Hc   30°51'

DECLINATION (15°–29°) CONTRARY NAME TO LATITUDE

N. Lat. {LHA greater than 180°...... Zn=Z / LHA less than 180°...... Zn=360–Z

S. Lat. {LHA greater than 180°...... Zn=180–Z / LHA less than 180°...... Zn=180+Z

LHA	15° Hc d Z	16° Hc d Z	17° Hc d Z	18° Hc d Z	19° Hc d Z	20° Hc d Z	21° Hc d Z	22° Hc d Z	23° Hc d Z	24° Hc d Z	25° Hc d Z	26° Hc d Z	27° Hc d Z	28° Hc d Z	29° Hc d Z	LHA
69	10 59 −40 117	10 19 39 118	09 38 40 119	08 57 39 119	08 17 40 120	07 36 39 121	06 55 39 121	06 13 40 122	05 32 40 123	04 51 40 123	04 09 40 124	03 27 40 125	02 46 41 125	02 05 40 126	01 24 41 127	69
68	11 25 41 117	10 44 40 118	10 03 40 119	09 22 40 119	08 41 40 120	08 01 41 121	07 20 41 121	06 38 40 122	05 57 41 123	05 16 41 123	04 34 40 124	03 52 41 125	03 11 41 125	02 30 41 126	01 49 42 126	68
67	11 50 41 116	11 09 40 117	10 28 41 118	09 47 40 119	09 06 40 120	08 26 41 120	07 44 41 121	07 03 41 122	06 22 41 122	05 41 41 123	04 59 41 124	04 17 41 125	03 36 42 125	02 54 41 126	02 13 42 126	67
66	12 14 42 116	11 33 41 117	10 52 41 118	10 11 41 118	09 30 40 119	08 50 42 120	08 08 41 121	07 27 42 122	06 45 41 122	06 04 42 123	05 22 41 124	04 41 42 124	03 59 42 125	03 17 42 126	02 35 42 126	66
65	12 39 42 115	11 57 41 116	11 16 42 117	10 35 42 118	09 53 41 119	09 13 42 120	08 31 42 120	07 49 42 121	07 08 42 122	06 26 42 123	05 44 42 123	05 02 42 124	04 20 42 125	03 38 42 125	02 56 43 126	65
64	13 02 42 115	12 21 42 116	11 39 42 117	10 58 42 117	10 16 41 118	09 35 42 119	08 54 43 120	08 11 42 121	07 30 43 121	06 48 42 122	06 06 43 123	05 23 42 124	04 41 43 124	03 58 42 125	03 16 43 126	64
63	13 26 43 114	12 44 42 115	12 03 43 116	11 20 42 117	10 39 43 118	09 56 42 119	09 16 43 119	08 33 43 120	07 51 43 121	07 09 43 122	06 27 43 122	05 44 43 123	05 01 42 124	04 19 43 125	03 36 43 125	63
62	13 49 43 114	13 06 42 114	12 25 43 115	11 43 43 116	11 00 42 117	10 18 43 118	09 37 44 119	08 53 43 120	08 11 43 120	07 30 44 121	06 48 44 122	06 04 43 123	05 21 43 123	04 38 43 124	03 55 44 125	62
61	14 11 43 113	13 28 43 114	12 46 43 115	12 03 43 116	11 21 43 116	10 38 43 117	09 57 44 118	09 14 44 119	08 30 43 120	07 47 44 120	07 05 44 121	06 21 44 122	05 37 43 123	04 54 44 124	04 10 44 125	61
60	14 30 43 113	13 50 43 113	13 07 44 114	12 23 43 115	11 41 44 116	10 57 43 117	10 14 44 118	09 33 44 119	08 49 44 119	08 05 44 120	07 22 45 121	06 38 44 122	05 54 44 122	05 10 44 123	04 26 45 124	60
59	14 50 44 112	14 06 43 113	13 24 44 114	12 40 43 115	11 57 44 115	11 13 43 116	10 30 45 117	09 45 44 118	09 01 44 119	08 17 45 120	07 32 44 120	06 48 45 121	06 03 44 122	05 19 45 123	04 34 45 124	59
58	15 10 44 111	14 26 44 112	13 42 44 113	12 58 44 114	12 14 44 115	11 30 44 116	10 46 45 116	10 01 44 117	09 17 45 118	08 32 45 119	07 47 45 120	07 02 45 120	06 17 45 121	05 32 45 122	04 47 45 123	58
57	15 31 45 111	14 46 44 112	14 02 45 113	13 17 44 113	12 33 45 114	11 48 45 115	11 03 45 116	10 18 45 116	09 33 45 117	08 48 46 118	08 02 45 119	07 17 46 120	06 31 45 121	05 46 46 121	05 00 46 122	57
56	15 51 45 110	15 06 45 111	14 21 45 112	13 36 45 113	12 51 45 114	12 06 45 115	11 21 46 115	10 35 45 116	09 50 46 117	09 04 46 118	08 18 46 118	07 32 46 119	06 46 46 120	06 00 46 121	05 14 46 122	56
55	16 11 45 109	15 26 46 110	14 40 45 111	13 55 46 112	13 09 46 113	12 23 46 114	11 37 46 115	10 51 46 115	10 05 46 116	09 19 46 117	08 33 46 118	07 47 47 119	07 00 46 119	06 14 47 120	05 27 47 121	55
54	16 33 46 109	15 47 46 110	15 01 46 111	14 15 46 111	13 29 46 112	12 43 46 113	11 57 47 114	11 10 46 115	10 24 47 115	09 37 46 116	08 51 47 117	08 04 47 118	07 17 47 119	06 30 47 120	05 43 47 120	54
53	16 51 46 108	16 05 46 109	15 19 46 110	14 33 47 111	13 46 46 112	13 00 47 112	12 13 47 113	11 26 47 114	10 39 47 115	09 52 47 116	09 05 47 116	08 18 48 117	07 30 47 118	06 43 48 119	05 55 47 120	53
52	17 12 47 107	16 25 46 108	15 39 47 109	14 52 47 110	14 05 47 111	13 18 47 112	12 31 48 112	11 43 47 113	10 56 48 114	10 08 47 115	09 21 48 116	08 33 48 116	07 45 48 117	06 57 48 118	06 09 48 119	52
51	17 30 47 106	16 43 47 107	15 56 47 108	15 09 47 109	14 22 47 110	13 35 48 111	12 47 48 112	11 59 47 113	11 12 48 113	10 24 48 114	09 36 48 115	08 48 48 116	08 00 48 116	07 11 49 117	06 22 48 118	51
50	17 53 48 106	17 05 47 107	16 18 48 108	15 30 48 108	14 42 48 109	13 54 48 110	13 06 48 111	12 18 48 112	11 30 49 112	10 41 48 113	09 53 49 114	09 04 49 115	08 15 48 116	07 27 49 117	06 38 49 118	50
49	18 08 48 105	17 20 48 106	16 32 48 107	15 44 48 108	14 56 48 108	14 08 49 109	13 19 48 110	12 31 49 111	11 42 49 112	10 53 49 113	10 05 49 113	09 16 49 114	08 27 50 115	07 37 49 116	06 48 50 117	49
48	18 26 48 104	17 38 49 105	16 49 48 106	16 01 49 107	15 12 49 108	14 23 49 109	13 34 49 110	12 45 49 110	11 56 50 111	11 06 49 112	10 17 50 113	09 27 49 114	08 38 50 115	07 48 50 115	06 58 50 116	48
47	18 46 49 103	17 57 49 104	17 08 49 105	16 19 49 106	15 30 49 107	14 41 50 108	13 51 49 109	13 02 50 110	12 12 50 110	11 22 50 111	10 32 50 112	09 42 50 113	08 52 51 114	08 01 50 115	07 11 51 116	47
46	19 04 49 102	18 15 49 103	17 26 50 104	16 36 49 105	15 47 50 106	14 57 50 107	14 07 50 108	13 17 50 109	12 27 51 110	11 36 50 110	10 46 51 111	09 55 50 112	09 05 51 113	08 14 51 114	07 23 51 115	46
45	19 23 50 101	18 33 49 102	17 44 50 103	16 54 50 104	16 04 50 105	15 14 50 106	14 24 51 107	13 33 50 108	12 43 51 109	11 52 51 110	11 01 51 110	10 10 51 111	09 19 52 112	08 27 51 113	07 36 52 114	45
44	19 40 50 100	18 50 50 101	18 00 50 102	17 10 50 103	16 20 51 104	15 29 50 105	14 39 51 106	13 48 51 107	12 57 51 108	12 06 51 109	11 15 52 109	10 23 51 110	09 32 52 111	08 40 52 112	07 48 52 113	44
43	19 58 50 099	19 08 51 100	18 17 50 101	17 27 51 102	16 36 51 103	15 45 51 104	14 54 51 105	14 03 51 106	13 12 52 107	12 20 51 108	11 29 52 108	10 37 52 109	09 45 52 110	08 53 52 111	08 01 53 112	43
42	20 14 51 098	19 23 50 099	18 33 51 100	17 42 51 101	16 51 51 102	16 00 52 103	15 08 51 104	14 17 52 105	13 25 52 106	12 33 52 107	11 41 52 107	10 49 53 108	09 56 52 109	09 04 53 110	08 11 53 111	42
41	20 31 51 097	19 40 51 098	18 49 51 099	17 58 51 100	17 06 51 101	16 15 52 102	15 23 52 103	14 31 52 104	13 39 52 105	12 47 53 106	11 54 52 106	11 02 53 107	10 09 53 108	09 16 53 109	08 23 54 110	41
40	20 47 51 096	19 56 52 097	19 04 51 098	18 13 52 099	17 21 52 100	16 29 52 101	15 37 52 102	14 45 53 103	13 52 52 104	13 00 53 105	12 07 53 105	11 14 53 106	10 21 53 107	09 28 54 108	08 34 53 109	40
39	21 02 52 095	20 10 51 096	19 19 52 097	18 27 52 098	17 35 52 099	16 43 53 100	15 50 52 101	14 58 53 102	14 05 53 103	13 12 53 104	12 19 53 104	11 26 54 105	10 32 53 106	09 39 54 107	08 45 54 108	39
38	21 17 52 094	20 25 52 095	19 33 52 096	18 41 53 097	17 48 52 098	16 56 53 099	16 03 53 100	15 10 53 101	14 17 53 102	13 24 54 103	12 30 53 103	11 37 54 104	10 43 54 105	09 49 54 106	08 55 55 107	38
37	21 33 53 093	20 40 52 094	19 48 53 095	18 55 53 096	18 02 53 097	17 09 53 098	16 16 53 099	15 23 54 100	14 29 53 101	13 36 54 102	12 42 54 102	11 48 54 103	10 54 54 104	10 00 55 105	09 05 54 106	37
36	21 46 53 092	20 53 52 093	20 01 53 094	19 08 53 095	18 15 53 096	17 22 54 097	16 28 53 098	15 35 54 099	14 41 54 100	13 47 54 101	12 53 54 101	11 59 55 102	11 04 54 103	10 10 55 104	09 15 55 105	36
35	22 00 53 091	21 07 53 092	20 14 53 093	19 21 54 094	18 27 53 095	17 34 54 095	16 40 54 096	15 46 54 097	14 52 55 098	13 57 54 099	13 03 55 100	12 08 54 101	11 14 55 102	10 19 55 103	09 24 56 104	35
34	22 13 54 090	21 19 53 091	20 26 53 092	19 33 54 093	18 39 54 094	17 45 54 094	16 51 54 095	15 57 55 096	15 02 54 097	14 08 55 098	13 13 55 099	12 18 55 100	11 23 55 101	10 28 56 102	09 32 55 103	34
33	22 25 54 089	21 31 53 089	20 38 54 090	19 44 54 091	18 50 54 092	17 56 55 093	17 01 54 094	16 07 55 095	15 12 55 096	14 17 55 097	13 22 55 098	12 27 56 099	11 31 55 100	10 36 56 101	09 40 56 102	33
32	22 37 54 088	21 43 54 089	20 49 54 090	19 55 55 091	19 00 54 091	18 06 55 092	17 11 55 093	16 16 55 094	15 21 55 095	14 26 56 096	13 30 55 097	12 35 56 098	11 39 56 099	10 43 56 100	09 47 56 101	32
31	22 48 54 087	21 54 54 088	21 00 55 089	20 05 54 090	19 11 55 091	18 16 55 091	17 21 55 092	16 26 56 093	15 30 55 094	14 35 56 095	13 39 56 096	12 43 56 097	11 47 56 098	10 51 57 099	09 54 56 100	31
30	22 58 54 086	22 04 55 087	21 09 54 088	20 15 55 088	19 20 55 089	18 25 55 090	17 30 56 091	16 34 55 092	15 39 56 093	14 43 56 094	13 47 56 095	12 51 57 096	11 54 56 097	10 58 57 098	10 01 57 099	30
29	23 08 55 085	22 13 54 086	21 19 55 087	20 24 55 087	19 29 55 088	18 34 56 089	17 38 55 090	16 43 56 091	15 47 56 092	14 51 56 093	13 55 57 094	12 58 57 095	12 02 57 096	11 05 57 097	10 08 58 098	29
28	23 17 55 084	22 22 55 084	21 27 55 085	20 32 56 086	19 36 55 087	18 41 56 088	17 45 56 089	16 49 56 090	15 53 56 091	14 57 57 092	14 00 56 093	13 04 57 094	12 07 57 095	11 10 58 096	10 12 57 097	28
27	23 25 55 083	22 30 55 083	21 35 55 084	20 40 56 085	19 44 56 086	18 48 56 087	17 52 56 088	16 56 57 089	15 59 56 090	15 03 57 091	14 06 57 092	13 09 58 093	12 11 57 094	11 14 58 095	10 16 58 095	27
26	23 34 56 081	22 38 55 082	21 43 56 083	20 47 56 084	19 51 56 085	18 55 57 086	17 58 56 087	17 02 57 088	16 05 57 089	15 08 57 089	14 11 57 090	13 14 58 091	12 16 58 092	11 18 58 093	10 20 59 094	26
25	23 41 55 080	22 46 56 081	21 50 56 082	20 54 56 083	19 58 57 084	19 01 56 085	18 05 57 086	17 08 57 087	16 11 57 088	15 14 58 089	14 16 57 089	13 18 58 090	12 20 58 091	11 22 58 092	10 24 59 093	25
24	23 49 56 079	22 53 56 080	21 57 56 081	21 01 57 082	20 04 56 083	19 08 57 084	18 11 57 085	17 14 58 086	16 16 57 087	15 19 58 088	14 21 58 088	13 23 59 089	12 24 58 090	11 26 59 091	10 27 59 092	24
23	23 56 56 078	23 00 56 079	22 04 57 080	21 07 57 081	20 10 57 082	19 13 57 083	18 16 57 084	17 19 58 085	16 21 57 085	15 24 58 086	14 26 58 087	13 27 58 088	12 29 59 089	11 30 59 090	10 31 59 091	23
22	24 02 56 077	23 06 56 078	22 10 57 079	21 13 57 080	20 16 57 081	19 19 58 082	18 21 57 083	17 24 58 084	16 26 58 084	15 28 58 085	14 30 59 086	13 31 59 087	12 32 59 088	11 33 59 089	10 34 60 090	22
21	24 09 57 076	23 12 56 077	22 16 57 078	21 19 57 078	20 22 58 079	19 24 57 080	18 27 58 081	17 29 58 082	16 31 58 083	15 33 59 084	14 34 58 085	13 36 60 086	12 36 59 087	11 37 60 088	10 37 60 089	21
20	24 15 57 075	23 18 57 075	22 21 57 076	21 24 57 077	20 27 58 078	19 29 58 079	18 31 57 080	17 34 59 081	16 35 58 082	15 37 59 083	14 38 59 083	13 39 59 084	12 40 60 085	11 40 60 086	10 40 60 087	20
19	24 20 57 073	23 23 57 074	22 26 57 075	21 29 58 076	20 31 57 077	19 34 58 078	18 36 58 079	17 38 58 080	16 40 59 080	15 41 59 081	14 42 59 082	13 43 60 083	12 43 60 084	11 43 60 085	10 43 60 086	19
18	24 25 57 072	23 28 57 073	22 31 58 074	21 33 57 075	20 36 58 076	19 38 58 077	18 40 58 078	17 42 59 079	16 43 59 079	15 44 59 080	14 45 59 081	13 46 60 082	12 46 60 083	11 46 60 084	10 46 60 085	18
17	24 30 57 071	23 33 58 072	22 35 58 073	21 37 57 074	20 40 58 075	19 42 58 076	18 44 59 077	17 45 58 077	16 47 59 078	15 48 60 079	14 48 59 080	13 49 60 081	12 49 60 082	11 49 60 083	10 49 60 084	17
16	24 34 58 070	23 36 57 071	22 39 58 072	21 41 58 073	20 43 58 074	19 45 58 074	18 47 59 075	17 48 58 076	16 50 59 077	15 51 60 078	14 51 59 079	13 52 60 079	12 52 60 080	11 52 60 081	10 52 60 082	16
15	24 38 58 069	23 40 57 070	22 43 58 071	21 45 58 072	20 47 58 072	19 49 59 073	18 50 58 074	17 52 59 075	16 53 59 076	15 54 60 077	14 54 60 077	13 54 60 078	12 54 60 079	11 54 60 080	10 54 60 081	15
14	24 41 58 067	23 43 57 068	22 46 58 069	21 48 58 070	20 50 59 071	19 51 58 072	18 53 59 073	17 54 59 073	16 55 59 074	15 56 60 075	14 56 60 076	13 56 60 077	12 56 60 078	11 56 60 079	10 56 60 079	14
13	24 44 58 066	23 46 58 067	22 48 58 068	21 50 58 069	20 52 58 069	19 54 59 070	18 55 59 071	17 56 59 072	16 57 60 073	15 57 59 074	14 58 60 074	13 58 60 075	12 58 60 076	11 58 60 077	10 58 60 078	13
12	24 47 58 064	23 49 58 065	22 51 58 066	21 53 59 067	20 54 58 068	19 56 59 069	18 57 59 070	17 58 59 070	16 59 60 071	16 00 60 072	15 00 60 073	14 00 60 074	13 00 60 075	12 00 60 075	11 00 60 076	12
11	24 49 59 063	23 51 58 064	22 53 58 065	21 55 59 066	20 56 58 066	19 58 59 067	18 59 59 068	18 00 60 069	17 00 59 070	16 01 60 071	15 01 60 071	14 01 60 072	13 01 60 073	12 01 60 074	11 01 60 075	11
10	24 51 58 062	23 53 58 063	22 55 59 064	21 56 58 064	20 58 59 065	19 59 59 066	19 00 59 067	18 01 59 068	17 02 60 068	16 02 60 069	15 02 60 070	14 02 60 071	13 02 60 072	12 02 60 073	11 02 60 073	10
9	24 52 58 061	23 54 58 061	22 56 59 062	21 58 59 063	20 59 59 064	20 00 59 065	19 01 59 065	18 02 60 066	17 02 59 067	16 03 60 068	15 03 60 069	14 03 60 069	13 03 60 070	12 03 60 071	11 03 60 072	9
8	24 54 59 059	23 55 58 060	22 57 59 061	21 59 59 062	21 00 59 062	20 01 59 063	19 02 60 064	18 02 59 065	17 03 60 066	16 04 60 066	15 04 60 067	14 04 60 068	13 04 60 069	12 04 60 069	11 04 60 070	8
7	24 55 59 058	23 56 58 059	22 58 59 059	21 59 58 060	21 01 60 061	20 02 59 062	19 02 59 063	18 03 60 063	17 04 60 064	16 04 59 065	15 05 60 066	14 05 60 066	13 05 60 067	12 05 60 068	11 05 60 069	7
6	24 56 59 056	23 57 58 057	22 59 59 058	22 00 59 059	21 01 59 059	20 02 59 060	19 03 60 061	18 04 60 062	17 05 60 062	16 05 60 063	15 05 60 064	14 05 60 065	13 05 60 065	12 06 60 066	11 06 60 067	6
5	24 57 59 055	23 58 59 055	22 59 58 056	22 01 59 057	21 02 59 058	20 03 60 058	19 04 60 059	18 04 60 060	17 05 60 061	16 06 60 061	15 06 60 062	14 06 60 063	13 06 60 064	12 07 60 064	11 07 60 065	5
4	24 58 59 054	23 58 58 054	23 00 59 055	22 01 59 055	21 02 59 056	20 03 59 057	19 04 60 057	18 05 60 058	17 05 60 059	16 06 60 059	15 07 60 060	14 07 60 061	13 07 60 062	12 07 60 062	11 07 60 063	4
3	24 58 59 052	23 59 59 053	23 00 59 053	22 02 60 054	21 03 60 054	20 04 60 055	19 04 60 056	18 05 60 056	17 06 60 057	16 07 60 058	15 07 60 058	14 07 60 059	13 07 60 060	12 08 60 060	11 08 60 061	3
2	24 59 59 051	23 59 59 051	23 01 60 052	22 02 59 052	21 03 59 053	20 04 60 053	19 05 60 054	18 05 60 055	17 06 60 055	16 07 60 056	15 07 60 056	14 08 60 057	13 08 60 058	12 08 60 058	11 08 60 059	2
1	24 59 59 049	24 00 59 050	23 01 60 050	22 02 59 051	21 03 60 051	20 04 60 052	19 05 60 052	18 06 60 053	17 06 60 054	16 07 60 054	15 08 60 055	14 08 60 055	13 08 60 056	12 08 60 057	11 08 60 057	1
0	25 00 60 048	24 00 60 048	23 01 60 049	22 02 60 049	21 03 60 050	20 04 60 050	19 05 60 051	18 06 60 051	17 06 60 052	16 08 60 053	15 08 60 053	14 08 60 054	13 08 60 054	12 09 60 055	11 08 60 056	0

| | 15° Zn=Z Zn=360−Z | 16° | 17° | 18° | 19° | 20° | 21° | 22° | 23° Zn=180−Z Zn=180+Z | 24° | 25° | 26° | 27° | 28° | 29° | |

DECLINATION (15°–29°) CONTRARY NAME TO LATITUDE

L.H.A. 36°

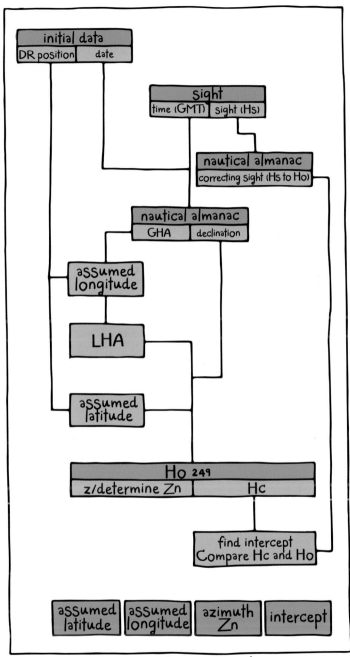

Sight Reduction Flowchart.

Now we can find our intercept by subtracting the Ho from the Hc:

Hc   30°51'
– Ho   30°48'
Intercept is 3 nautical miles away

We know the intercept is away from the GP of the sun by recalling the formula Ho Mo To which means Ho is greater than Hc then we are closer to the GP. In this case the Ho is less than the Hc, so we are further away.

Now what about our bearing? We know we took an afternoon observation and a Z would indicate that the sun is in the east. We know that is impossible so we consult the instructions at the top of the page that tells us if the LHA is less than 180° then Zn = 360°-Z. So we have the following

        360°
–   147°
Zn 213°, which makes sense

This is standard procedure for finding Intercept.

The declination correction is always factored—either added or subtracted—from the Hc to get exact Hc for the time of the sight.

Let's review what you just did. We are always looking for the GP of the sun at the exact time of our observation. The tables can only be entered with whole numbers of degrees, so we have to make allowance for the minutes of declination. We use Table 5 for this and then either add or subtract that number to the Hc to arrive at the final Hc, or calculated altitude.

Since we already established the relationship between sextant angle and the distance from the GP in this first diagram, we know that the Ho is greater than the Hc, so we must be closer by x to the GP. The rule to remember is Ho Mo To, which means Ho is more than the Hc; it's toward the GP.

If the Hc is larger (see diagram on page 42), then we are farther away. The distance we are either closer to or farther from the GP after we compare our Ho to the Hc is called the intercept.

The Noon Sight

For many generations ship captains navigated—during the great days of sailing ships in the mid-nineteenth to the turn of the twentieth century—using only the tried and true method of finding latitude at Local Apparent Noon (LAN), known as the noon sight, when the sun is on the observer's meridian. This was sometimes the only observation that square-rigged captains did. It is relatively easy, requires little math, and is not dependent on an accurate timepiece. There are plenty of long distance sailors today who just use this sight, and no others. Once the latitude is found, mariners just dead reckon along their course until noon the next day. Noon sight can be easily done without a great deal of fuss and fanfare, and is an effective means of finding latitude. As a matter of fact, the celestial day at sea always began at noon—or eight bells, as it is also called. Remember, before GPS and the simplified tables that we now use, many mariners sailed down the latitudes for a certain distance and then would either turn north or south depending on the DR to arrive at their destination. Of course, this method had its downside. If the sky is overcast and the sun not visible, then the noon sight is for naught. So the old mariners would proceed just using the DR. But if the sun is visible, the noon sight is a great technique and is one of the three sun sights that the navigator should take daily. One note here about the noon sight: I am here only showing its basic method. There are techniques that can be used to actually find longitude using the noon sight, and with the use of an accurate timepiece a fix can be obtained. But that information can be learned on your own. For the time being, let's focus on the basic simple combination of finding latitude using LAN.

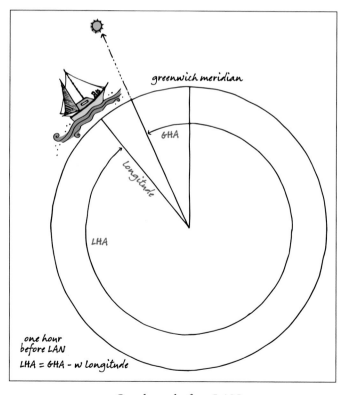

One hour before LAN.

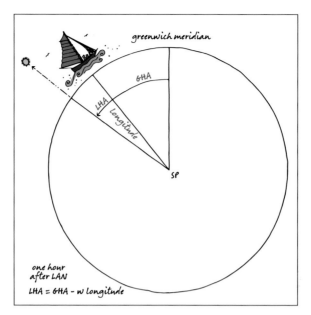

One hour after LAN.

Basically, what we are solving for is the GP of the sun when it is over the meridian of our vessel. The diagram below shows how this looks.

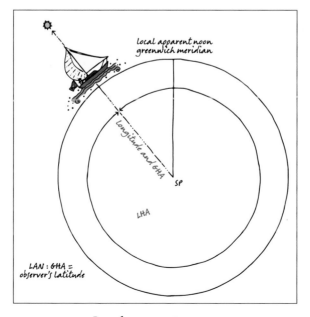

Local apparent noon.

If you examine the diagram above, you can tell from the time of local hour noon that the GHA is exactly the same as the longitude of the observer. Here it is essential to recall that in west longitude GHA minus longitude equals LHA, and that is another definition of local noon is when the LHA is 0°. Look at the diagram and make sure you understand what I am saying.

So how do we calculate the time of LAN? The apparent sun is moving at four miles every minute of time. So even though on land noon is calculated at 12:00 p.m., at sea the exact time of the sun passing over our meridian may be before or after 12:00 p.m. Our job is to first calculate what time the sun will pass overhead where we are. Once again, we turn to the ever reliable *Nautical Almanac.* Let's go to October 31, 2015 (please turn to page 105). We are at a DR 35°25' by W 68°15'. We want to calculate the time local noon will occur where we are.

At the bottom right of the daily sun pages, you'll see a section called "Sun," which lists the day, equation of time, and then a column called "Mer. Passage." This final column is what we are interested in. The tables tell us that on the 31st, the meridian passage of the sun, in other words when the sun will be over the Greenwich meridian, would occur at 11:44. Now that is local time at Greenwich.

But we are not at Greenwich; we are 68°15 west of Greenwich, and we want to know how long it will take the sun to reach our meridian. And we want to know that time in GMT. Therefore, we must do some calculations to find the exact time of local noon based on our DR. This is not as difficult as it may sound, for there are tables which do all the hard work for us. Here's how it is done:

We have a DR of N 35°25' by W 68°15'. For time of meridian passage, we are only interested in the longitude of our DR. (See table on page 64.) What we want to do is find the time in GMT for local noon for our DR longitude. We see that the tables tell us that local time for meridian passage is 11:44. Now that is true if, once again, we are at the Greenwich meridian, or at the central meridians of each time zone, i.e., 15°, 30°, 45°, etc. This time, by the way, is the local time of the observer. But we are not. We are—or we think we are—at W 68°15' of Greenwich. So go to page i at the rear of the *Nautical Almanac* to a table marked "Conversion of Arc to Time" (please turn to page 110). This table lists the relationship of arc to time, or how far the sun has traveled in a period of time. For instance, you could look down the left-hand column to 15° and see that, yes, it takes the sun one hour to travel 15°.

Now, look up our DR longitude of 68° and see that it has taken the sun 4 hours and 32 minutes to move that distance. That makes sense, right? The sun is moving at 15° an hour. And then if we go to the right-hand column for minutes of arc we see that it has taken another one minute of time to move 15' of arc. So we add four hours and thirty-two minutes plus 1' and we get four hours and thirty-three minutes. So we know it takes the sun four hours and thirty-three minutes to move westward from Greenwich to our DR longitude of W 68°15'.

Okay. Now we want to convert our local time to GMT. So take the meridian passage of time 11:44 LMT and add to that four hours and thirty-three minutes. You get 16:17 GMT for the time the sun would be at the meridian for

68°15' minutes at our calculated DR. Remember, this time is in GMT and not local time so don't be scratching your head thinking how can noon be at this time.

Note: What we are really doing above is converting arc to time (please refer to page 110). We know this relationship exists so in order to find out what exact time it is for LAN, convert our DR longitude to the time it takes the sun to move from Greenwich in a westward direction. Once you know how long it takes the sun to move to the DR longitude, we add that time to the time of meridian passage and get our time for meridian passage for GMT at the longitude for our DR position.

So now you're up on deck about twenty minutes or so before LAN with a sextant. Check the index error. Now, put your sun screens down and begin taking a series of shots of the lower limb of the sun.

Take a couple of shots every minute or two and the altitude will be increasing. In other words, the sun has not yet reached our meridian. We don't have to record these numbers, just observe that the sun is getting higher in the sky. (The term a.m., by the way, refers to "ante meridian," which means before the meridian.) Finally, there will come a moment when it looks as if the sun has stopped rising and will hang in the same spot for a half a minute or so. That is its highest spot. Mark the Hs, wait a few moments, and then take another shot and the altitude should begin to decrease. Take another couple of observations just to make certain.

2015 OCT. 31, NOV. 1, 2 (SAT., SUN., MON.) 213

UT	SUN GHA	Dec	MOON GHA	v	Dec	d	HP
31 00	184 05.3	S13 55.6	314 29.7	7.1	N18 09.9	1.0	58.5
01	199 05.3	56.4	328 55.8	7.2	18 10.9	0.8	58.5
02	214 05.3	57.2	343 22.0	7.2	18 11.7	0.8	58.4
03	229 05.4	.. 58.0	357 48.2	7.2	18 12.5	0.6	58.4
04	244 05.4	58.8	12 14.4	7.4	18 13.1	0.5	58.4
05	259 05.4	13 59.6	26 40.8	7.3	18 13.6	0.4	58.3
06	274 05.5	S14 00.4	41 07.1	7.4	N18 14.0	0.2	58.3
S 07	289 05.5	01.3	55 33.5	7.5	18 14.2	0.2	58.2
A 08	304 05.5	02.1	70 00.0	7.5	18 14.4	0.1	58.2
T 09	319 05.6	.. 02.9	84 26.5	7.5	18 14.5	0.1	58.2
U 10	334 05.6	03.7	98 53.0	7.7	18 14.4	0.2	58.1
R 11	349 05.6	04.5	113 19.7	7.6	18 14.2	0.3	58.1
D 12	4 05.6	S14 05.3	127 46.3	7.7	N18 13.9	0.3	58.0
A 13	19 05.7	06.1	142 13.0	7.8	18 13.6	0.5	58.0
Y 14	34 05.7	06.9	156 39.8	7.8	18 13.1	0.7	58.0
15	49 05.7	.. 07.7	171 06.6	7.9	18 12.4	0.7	57.9
16	64 05.7	08.5	185 33.5	8.0	18 11.7	0.8	57.9
17	79 05.8	09.4	200 00.5	8.0	18 10.9	0.9	57.8
18	94 05.8	S14 10.2	214 27.5	8.0	N18 10.0	1.1	57.8
19	109 05.8	11.0	228 54.5	8.2	18 08.9	1.1	57.8
20	124 05.8	11.8	243 21.7	8.1	18 07.8	1.3	57.7
21	139 05.9	.. 12.6	257 48.8	8.3	18 06.5	1.3	57.7
22	154 05.9	13.4	272 16.1	8.3	18 05.2	1.5	57.6
23	169 05.9	14.2	286 43.4	8.3	18 03.7	1.5	57.6
1 00	184 05.9	S14 15.0	301 10.7	8.5	N18 02.2	1.7	57.6
01	199 06.0	15.8	315 38.2	8.4	18 00.5	1.8	57.5
02	214 06.0	16.6	330 05.6	8.6	17 58.7	1.8	57.5
03	229 06.0	.. 17.4	344 33.2	8.6	17 56.9	2.0	57.4
04	244 06.0	18.2	359 00.8	8.7	17 54.9	2.1	57.4
05	259 06.0	19.0	13 28.5	8.7	17 52.8	2.2	57.4
06	274 06.1	S14 19.8	27 56.2	8.8	N17 50.6	2.2	57.3
S 07	289 06.1	20.6	42 24.0	8.9	17 48.4	2.4	57.3
U 08	304 06.1	21.4	56 51.9	8.9	17 46.0	2.5	57.3
N 09	319 06.1	.. 22.2	71 19.8	9.0	17 43.5	2.5	57.2
D 10	334 06.1	23.0	85 47.8	9.0	17 41.0	2.7	57.2
A 11	349 06.2	23.8	100 15.8	9.2	17 38.3	2.7	57.1
Y 12	4 06.2	S14 24.6	114 44.0	9.1	N17 35.6	2.9	57.1
13	19 06.2	25.4	129 12.1	9.3	17 32.7	2.9	57.1
14	34 06.2	26.2	143 40.4	9.3	17 29.8	3.0	57.0
15	49 06.2	.. 27.0	158 08.7	9.4	17 26.8	3.2	57.0
16	64 06.2	27.8	172 37.1	9.5	17 23.6	3.2	56.9
17	79 06.3	28.6	187 05.6	9.5	17 20.4	3.3	56.9
18	94 06.3	S14 29.4	201 34.1	9.6	N17 17.1	3.4	56.9
19	109 06.3	30.2	216 02.7	9.6	17 13.7	3.5	56.8
20	124 06.3	31.0	230 31.3	9.7	17 10.2	3.6	56.8
21	139 06.3	.. 31.8	245 00.0	9.8	17 06.6	3.6	56.8
22	154 06.3	32.6	259 28.8	9.9	17 03.0	3.8	56.7
23	169 06.4	33.4	273 57.7	9.9	16 59.2	3.8	56.7
2 00	184 06.4	S14 34.2	288 26.6	10.0	N16 55.4	4.0	56.7
01	199 06.4	35.0	302 55.6	10.0	16 51.4	4.0	56.6
02	214 06.4	35.8	317 24.6	10.2	16 47.4	4.1	56.6
03	229 06.4	.. 36.6	331 53.8	10.2	16 43.3	4.1	56.5
04	244 06.4	37.4	346 23.0	10.2	16 39.2	4.3	56.5
05	259 06.4	38.2	0 52.2	10.3	16 34.9	4.3	56.5
06	274 06.4	S14 39.0	15 21.5	10.4	N16 30.6	4.5	56.4
07	289 06.5	39.8	29 50.9	10.5	16 26.1	4.5	56.4
08	304 06.5	40.6	44 20.4	10.5	16 21.6	4.5	56.4
M 09	319 06.5	.. 41.4	58 49.9	10.6	16 17.1	4.7	56.3
O 10	334 06.5	42.2	73 19.5	10.7	16 12.4	4.8	56.3
N 11	349 06.5	43.0	87 49.2	10.7	16 07.6	4.8	56.3
D 12	4 06.5	S14 43.7	102 18.9	10.8	N16 02.8	4.9	56.2
A 13	19 06.5	44.5	116 48.7	10.9	15 57.9	4.9	56.2
Y 14	34 06.5	45.3	131 18.6	10.9	15 53.0	5.1	56.2
15	49 06.5	.. 46.1	145 48.5	11.0	15 47.9	5.1	56.1
16	64 06.6	46.9	160 18.5	11.1	15 42.8	5.2	56.1
17	79 06.6	47.7	174 48.6	11.1	15 37.6	5.3	56.1
18	94 06.6	S14 48.5	189 18.7	11.2	N15 32.3	5.3	56.0
19	109 06.6	49.3	203 48.9	11.3	15 27.0	5.4	56.0
20	124 06.6	50.1	218 19.2	11.3	15 21.6	5.5	56.0
21	139 06.6	.. 50.9	232 49.5	11.4	15 16.1	5.5	55.9
22	154 06.6	51.6	247 19.9	11.5	15 10.6	5.6	55.9
23	169 06.6	52.4	261 50.4	11.5	N15 05.0	5.7	55.9
	SD 16.1	d 0.8	SD 15.8		15.6		15.3

Twilight / Sunrise / Moonrise

Lat.	Naut.	Civil	Sunrise	Moonrise 31	1	2	3
N 72	06 05	07 28	08 54	▭	17 45	19 37	21 22
N 70	06 01	07 15	08 29	17 27	18 44	20 14	21 45
68	05 57	07 04	08 09	18 08	19 18	20 39	22 03
66	05 54	06 56	07 54	18 36	19 43	20 59	22 18
64	05 51	06 48	07 41	18 57	20 02	21 15	22 30
62	05 49	06 42	07 30	19 14	20 18	21 28	22 40
60	05 47	06 36	07 21	19 28	20 31	21 39	22 49
N 58	05 44	06 31	07 13	19 41	20 42	21 48	22 56
56	05 42	06 26	07 06	19 51	20 52	21 57	23 03
54	05 40	06 22	07 00	20 00	21 01	22 04	23 09
52	05 39	06 19	06 54	20 09	21 08	22 11	23 14
50	05 37	06 15	06 49	20 16	21 15	22 17	23 19
45	05 33	06 07	06 38	20 32	21 30	22 30	23 29
N 40	05 28	06 00	06 29	20 45	21 42	22 40	23 38
35	05 25	05 54	06 21	20 56	21 53	22 49	23 45
30	05 21	05 49	06 14	21 06	22 02	22 57	23 52
20	05 12	05 39	06 01	21 23	22 18	23 11	24 03
N 10	05 04	05 29	05 50	21 37	22 31	23 23	24 12
0	04 54	05 19	05 40	21 51	22 44	23 34	24 22
S 10	04 43	05 08	05 30	22 05	22 57	23 45	24 31
20	04 29	04 56	05 19	22 20	23 11	23 57	24 40
30	04 11	04 40	05 06	22 36	23 26	24 11	00 11
35	03 59	04 31	04 58	22 46	23 35	24 19	00 19
40	03 45	04 20	04 50	22 57	23 46	24 28	00 28
45	03 28	04 07	04 39	23 10	23 58	24 38	00 38
S 50	03 05	03 51	04 27	23 26	24 12	00 12	00 51
52	02 54	03 43	04 21	23 34	24 19	00 19	00 57
54	02 41	03 34	04 15	23 42	24 27	00 27	01 03
56	02 25	03 24	04 08	23 52	24 35	00 35	01 11
58	02 06	03 13	04 00	24 02	00 02	00 45	01 19
S 60	01 42	02 59	03 51	24 14	00 14	00 56	01 28

Sunset / Twilight / Moonset

Lat.	Sunset	Civil	Naut.	Moonset 31	1	2	3
N 72	14 31	15 58	17 21	▭	15 22	15 16	15 11
N 70	14 57	16 11	17 25	13 48	14 23	14 39	14 46
68	15 17	16 22	17 28	13 07	13 48	14 12	14 27
66	15 32	16 30	17 32	12 39	13 23	13 52	14 12
64	15 45	16 38	17 34	12 18	13 03	13 36	13 59
62	15 56	16 44	17 37	12 00	12 47	13 22	13 48
60	16 05	16 50	17 39	11 46	12 34	13 11	13 39
N 58	16 13	16 55	17 42	11 34	12 23	13 01	13 31
56	16 20	17 00	17 44	11 23	12 13	12 52	13 24
54	16 27	17 04	17 46	11 14	12 04	12 44	13 18
52	16 32	17 08	17 48	11 06	11 56	12 37	13 12
50	16 38	17 11	17 50	10 58	11 49	12 31	13 07
45	16 49	17 19	17 54	10 42	11 33	12 17	12 55
N 40	16 58	17 26	17 58	10 29	11 21	12 06	12 46
35	17 06	17 32	18 02	10 18	11 10	11 57	12 38
30	17 13	17 38	18 06	10 08	11 01	11 48	12 31
20	17 26	17 48	18 14	09 51	10 44	11 33	12 18
N 10	17 37	17 58	18 23	09 36	10 30	11 21	12 08
0	17 47	18 08	18 33	09 22	10 17	11 09	11 57
S 10	17 58	18 19	18 45	09 09	10 04	10 56	11 47
20	18 09	18 32	18 59	08 54	09 49	10 43	11 36
30	18 22	18 47	19 17	08 37	09 33	10 29	11 23
35	18 30	18 57	19 29	08 27	09 23	10 20	11 16
40	18 38	19 08	19 43	08 16	09 12	10 10	11 08
45	18 49	19 21	20 01	08 02	08 59	09 58	10 58
S 50	19 01	19 37	20 24	07 46	08 44	09 44	10 46
52	19 07	19 45	20 35	07 38	08 36	09 38	10 41
54	19 13	19 54	20 48	07 30	08 28	09 30	10 35
56	19 21	20 05	21 04	07 20	08 19	09 22	10 28
58	19 29	20 16	21 24	07 10	08 08	09 13	10 20
S 60	19 38	20 30	21 50	06 57	07 56	09 02	10 11

SUN / MOON

Day	Eqn. of Time 00h	12h	Mer. Pass.	Mer. Pass. Upper	Lower	Age	Phase
d	m s	m s	h m	h m	h m	d %	
31	16 21	16 22	11 44	03 09	15 37	18 79	
1	16 24	16 25	11 44	04 04	16 31	19 70	
2	16 25	16 26	11 44	04 56	17 21	20 60	

There are all kinds of add-ons you could do to this observation. But you want to keep it simple. Remember it is not necessary to work out the exact time, only the Hs of the observation. Following standard procedure, reduce the Hs to the HO by factoring in the height of eye, index error—if there is one, and the third correction. Once you reduce the Hs to the HO, follow a simple formula to find latitude:

Latitude = 90 degrees – HO = ZD + or – declination.

Now there are formulas for knowing whether you should add or subtract the declination, but common sense is your best guide here. As a rational person, you have an idea of where you are. In other words, think about what you are doing and forget the formulas. If you subtract the declination and find that all of a sudden you are in the Caribbean, when you know you are not, then add the declination.

The declination is taken for the hour. Remember that the declination is changing very slowly, so this brings only a minimal error. By definition, when the sun is over our meridian, its bearing is either 0° or 180°, depending on whether it is to the north or south. Since most of us sail in the northern or mid-latitudes, the sun will be 180°. In other words, the ZN will be 180°, and since our LOP is perpendicular to the bearing line, a Line of Position is an east-west line, known as a line of latitude.

And we know that when we plot the LOP it is always at right angles to the bearing, ergo, our LOP is a line of latitude. Pretty cool, huh? Some examples follow.

Noon sights have advantages in that accurate time is not necessary. The calculation is relatively easy, as is the plotting.

Example 1: On October 31, we are at a DR of N 35°12' by W 68°15'. Height of Eye is 10 feet. We are taking a lower limb shot. We want to find latitude. Our Hs is 40°26.1'.

Time of Meridian Passage	11:44	
Arc to time for 68°15'	4:33	
Time Mer. Pass GMT	16:17	

Hs	40°26.1'	Declination at 16000 hrs is
		S14°08.5'
– dip	3.1'	
App alt	40°23.0'	
+3rd corr	15.1'	
Ho	40°38.1'	

Latitude = 90° – Ho = ZD +/– declination so

	90°
-	40°38.1'
	49°21.9' ZD – Dec
-	14°08.5'
Lat N 35°13.4'	

2015 JULY 18, 19, 20 (SAT., SUN., MON.)   143

UT	SUN GHA	SUN Dec	MOON GHA	MOON v	MOON Dec	d	HP	Lat.	Naut.	Civil	Sunrise	Moonrise 18	19	20	21
d h	° ′	° ′	° ′	′	° ′	′	′	°	h m	h m	h m	h m	h m	h m	h m
18 00	178 27.3	N21 06.7	156 42.9	13.0	N12 08.4	7.4	54.9	N 72	□	□	□	05 09	06 48	08 22	09 55
01	193 27.2	06.3	171 14.9	13.2	12 01.0	7.5	54.9	N 70	□	□	□	05 29	07 00	08 28	09 56
02	208 27.2	05.8	185 47.1	13.1	11 53.5	7.5	54.9	68	////	////	00 41	05 45	07 10	08 33	09 56
03	223 27.1 ..	05.4	200 19.2	13.2	11 46.0	7.5	54.9	66	////	////	01 51	05 58	07 18	08 37	09 56
04	238 27.1	05.0	214 51.4	13.3	11 38.5	7.6	54.9	64	////	////	02 26	06 08	07 25	08 41	09 56
05	253 27.0	04.5	229 23.7	13.3	11 30.9	7.6	54.9	62	////	01 13	02 51	06 17	07 31	08 44	09 56
06	268 27.0	N21 04.1	243 56.0	13.4	N11 23.3	7.7	54.8	60	////	01 57	03 11	06 25	07 36	08 46	09 56
07	283 26.9	03.7	258 28.4	13.4	11 15.6	7.7	54.8	N 58	////	02 25	03 27	06 31	07 40	08 49	09 57
S 08	298 26.9	03.2	273 00.8	13.4	11 07.9	7.8	54.8	56	01 07	02 46	03 40	06 37	07 44	08 51	09 57
A 09	313 26.8 ..	02.8	287 33.2	13.5	11 00.1	7.8	54.8	54	01 47	03 03	03 52	06 42	07 48	08 52	09 57
T 10	328 26.8	02.3	302 05.7	13.6	10 52.3	7.9	54.8	52	02 13	03 18	04 02	06 47	07 51	08 54	09 57
U 11	343 26.7	01.9	316 38.3	13.6	10 44.4	7.9	54.8	50	02 33	03 30	04 12	06 51	07 54	08 56	09 57
R 12	358 26.7	N21 01.5	331 10.9	13.6	N10 36.5	7.9	54.8	45	03 10	03 55	04 33	07 01	08 00	08 59	09 57
D 13	13 26.7	01.0	345 43.5	13.7	10 28.6	8.0	54.7	N 40	03 36	04 15	04 47	07 08	08 05	09 02	09 57
A 14	28 26.6	00.6	0 16.2	13.7	10 20.6	8.0	54.7	35	03 56	04 31	05 00	07 15	08 10	09 04	09 57
Y 15	43 26.6	21 00.2	14 48.9	13.7	10 12.6	8.1	54.7	30	04 12	04 44	05 11	07 21	08 14	09 06	09 58
16	58 26.5	20 59.7	29 21.6	13.8	10 04.5	8.1	54.7	20	04 38	05 06	05 30	07 31	08 21	09 10	09 58
17	73 26.5	59.3	43 54.4	13.9	9 56.4	8.1	54.7	N 10	04 58	05 25	05 47	07 40	08 27	09 13	09 58
18	88 26.4	N20 58.8	58 27.3	13.9	N 9 48.3	8.2	54.7	0	05 15	05 41	06 03	07 48	08 33	09 16	09 58
19	103 26.4	58.4	73 00.2	13.9	9 40.1	8.2	54.6	S 10	05 30	05 56	06 18	07 56	08 38	09 19	09 58
20	118 26.3	57.9	87 33.1	14.0	9 31.9	8.2	54.6	20	05 44	06 11	06 34	08 05	08 44	09 22	09 59
21	133 26.3 ..	57.5	102 06.1	14.0	9 23.7	8.3	54.6	30	05 58	06 27	06 53	08 15	08 51	09 26	09 59
22	148 26.2	57.1	116 39.1	14.0	9 15.4	8.3	54.6	35	06 05	06 36	07 04	08 21	08 55	09 28	09 59
23	163 26.2	56.6	131 12.1	14.1	9 07.1	8.4	54.6	40	06 13	06 46	07 16	08 27	09 00	09 30	09 59
19 00	178 26.1	N20 56.2	145 45.2	14.1	N 8 58.7	8.4	54.6	45	06 22	06 58	07 31	08 35	09 05	09 33	09 59
01	193 26.1	55.7	160 18.3	14.2	8 50.3	8.4	54.6	S 50	06 31	07 11	07 48	08 44	09 11	09 36	10 00
02	208 26.0	55.3	174 51.5	14.2	8 41.9	8.4	54.6	52	06 35	07 18	07 57	08 48	09 14	09 37	10 00
03	223 26.0 ..	54.8	189 24.7	14.2	8 33.5	8.5	54.5	54	06 40	07 25	08 06	08 52	09 17	09 39	10 00
04	238 26.0	54.4	203 57.9	14.3	8 25.0	8.5	54.5	56	06 45	07 32	08 16	08 57	09 20	09 41	10 00
05	253 25.9	53.9	218 31.2	14.3	8 16.5	8.6	54.5	58	06 50	07 40	08 28	09 03	09 24	09 43	10 00
06	268 25.9	N20 53.5	233 04.5	14.4	N 8 07.9	8.6	54.5	S 60	06 56	07 50	08 42	09 09	09 28	09 45	10 00
07	283 25.8	53.0	247 37.9	14.4	7 59.3	8.6	54.5								
S 08	298 25.8	52.6	262 11.3	14.4	7 50.7	8.6	54.5	Lat.	Sunset	Civil	Naut.	Moonset 18	19	20	21
U 09	313 25.7 ..	52.1	276 44.7	14.4	7 42.1	8.7	54.5	°	h m	h m	h m	h m	h m	h m	h m
N 10	328 25.7	51.7	291 18.1	14.5	7 33.4	8.6	54.5	N 72	□	□	□	22 12	22 07	22 03	21 58
11	343 25.6	51.2	305 51.6	14.6	7 24.8	8.8	54.4	N 70	□	□	□	21 59	21 59	22 00	22 00
D 12	358 25.6	N20 50.8	320 25.2	14.5	N 7 16.0	8.7	54.4	68	23 20	////	////	21 47	21 53	21 58	22 02
A 13	13 25.6	50.3	334 58.7	14.6	7 07.3	8.8	54.4	66	22 18	////	////	21 38	21 48	21 56	22 03
Y 14	28 25.5	49.9	349 32.3	14.6	6 58.5	8.8	54.4	64	21 44	////	////	21 30	21 43	21 54	22 05
15	43 25.5 ..	49.4	4 05.9	14.7	6 49.7	8.8	54.4	62	21 20	22 54	////	21 24	21 39	21 53	22 06
16	58 25.4	48.9	18 39.6	14.6	6 40.9	8.8	54.4	60	21 00	22 13	////	21 18	21 35	21 51	22 07
17	73 25.4	48.5	33 13.2	14.8	6 32.1	8.9	54.4	N 58	20 44	21 46	////	21 12	21 32	21 50	22 08
18	88 25.4	N20 48.0	47 47.0	14.7	N 6 23.2	8.9	54.4	56	20 31	21 25	23 01	21 08	21 29	21 49	22 08
19	103 25.3	47.6	62 20.7	14.8	6 14.3	8.9	54.4	54	20 19	21 08	22 23	21 04	21 27	21 48	22 09
20	118 25.3	47.1	76 54.5	14.8	6 05.4	8.9	54.4	52	20 09	20 54	21 58	21 00	21 25	21 47	22 10
21	133 25.2 ..	46.7	91 28.3	14.8	5 56.5	8.9	54.3	50	20 00	20 41	21 38	20 56	21 22	21 47	22 10
22	148 25.2	46.2	106 02.1	14.8	5 47.6	9.0	54.3	45	19 41	20 16	21 02	20 49	21 18	21 45	22 12
23	163 25.1	45.7	120 35.9	14.9	5 38.6	9.0	54.3	N 40	19 26	19 57	20 36	20 43	21 14	21 44	22 13
20 00	178 25.1	N20 45.3	135 09.8	14.9	N 5 29.6	9.0	54.3	35	19 13	19 41	20 16	20 37	21 11	21 42	22 14
01	193 25.1	44.8	149 43.7	14.9	5 20.6	9.0	54.3	30	19 01	19 28	20 00	20 32	21 08	21 41	22 15
02	208 25.0	44.4	164 17.6	15.0	5 11.6	9.0	54.3	20	18 42	19 04	19 34	20 24	21 02	21 40	22 16
03	223 25.0 ..	43.9	178 51.6	15.0	5 02.6	9.1	54.3	N 10	18 25	18 48	19 14	20 17	20 58	21 38	22 17
04	238 24.9	43.4	193 25.6	15.0	4 53.5	9.1	54.3	0	18 10	18 32	18 58	20 10	20 54	21 36	22 18
05	253 24.9	43.0	207 59.6	15.0	4 44.4	9.1	54.3	S 10	17 55	18 17	18 43	20 03	20 49	21 35	22 20
06	268 24.9	N20 42.5	222 33.6	15.0	N 4 35.3	9.1	54.3	20	17 38	18 02	18 29	19 55	20 45	21 33	22 21
07	283 24.8	42.0	237 07.6	15.1	4 26.2	9.1	54.3	30	17 20	17 46	18 15	19 47	20 39	21 31	22 22
08	298 24.8	41.6	251 41.7	15.1	4 17.1	9.1	54.3	35	17 09	17 37	18 08	19 42	20 36	21 30	22 23
M 09	313 24.8 ..	41.1	266 15.8	15.1	4 08.0	9.2	54.3	40	16 57	17 26	18 00	19 36	20 33	21 28	22 24
O 10	328 24.7	40.6	280 49.9	15.1	3 58.8	9.1	54.2	45	16 42	17 15	17 51	19 29	20 28	21 27	22 25
N 11	343 24.7	40.2	295 24.0	15.1	3 49.7	9.2	54.2	S 50	16 25	17 02	17 42	19 21	20 24	21 25	22 26
D 12	358 24.6	N20 39.7	309 58.1	15.2	N 3 40.5	9.2	54.2	52	16 16	16 55	17 38	19 18	20 21	21 24	22 27
A 13	13 24.6	39.2	324 32.3	15.2	3 31.3	9.2	54.2	54	16 07	16 49	17 32	19 14	20 19	21 23	22 28
Y 14	28 24.6	38.8	339 06.5	15.2	3 22.1	9.2	54.2	56	15 57	16 41	17 28	19 09	20 16	21 22	22 28
15	43 24.5 ..	38.3	353 40.7	15.2	3 12.9	9.2	54.2	58	15 45	16 33	17 23	19 04	20 13	21 21	22 29
16	58 24.5	37.8	8 14.9	15.2	3 03.7	9.2	54.2	S 60	15 31	16 23	17 17	18 58	20 09	21 20	22 30
17	73 24.5	37.4	22 49.1	15.2	2 54.5	9.3	54.2								
18	88 24.4	N20 36.9	37 23.3	15.3	N 2 45.2	9.2	54.2			SUN			MOON		
19	103 24.4	36.4	51 57.6	15.3	2 36.0	9.3	54.2	Day	Eqn. of Time 00ʰ	12ʰ	Mer. Pass.	Mer. Pass. Upper	Lower	Age	Phase
20	118 24.4	35.9	66 31.9	15.3	2 26.7	9.2	54.2	d	m s	m s	h m	h m	h m	d	%
21	133 24.3 ..	35.5	81 06.2	15.2	2 17.5	9.3	54.2	18	06 11	06 13	12 06	13 59	01 36	02	6
22	148 24.3	35.0	95 40.4	15.3	2 08.2	9.3	54.2	19	06 15	06 18	12 06	14 43	02 21	03	11
23	163 24.3	34.5	110 14.7	15.4	N 1 58.9	9.3	54.2	20	06 19	06 21	12 06	15 26	03 05	04	18
	SD 15.8	d 0.5	SD 14.9		14.8		14.8								

Example 2: On July 20, the DR is N 24°13' by W 52°25'
Again the Height of Eye is 10 feet, we are taking a lower
limb shot and the Hs is 82°10.2'.

(see page 108)

Time Mer Pass   12:06 (ARC to Time)
Arc/time 52°25'   3:29:40
Time LAN   15:35:40 GMT   Declination at 1600 hrs
                                 N20°37.8'

Hs	86°10.2'
-dip	3.1
App alt	86°7.1'
3rd corr+	15.8'
Ho	86°22.9'

Latitude = 90° − Ho = ZD +/− Dec

90°	
-Ho	86°22.9'
ZD	3°37.1'
+ dec	20°37.8'
Lat	N 24°14.9'

I am rounding off the declination to 1600 hrs. Remember
we don't need to time this shot. Also notice that very rarely
will the LAN latitude match up to the one you thought you
were at on the DR. The discrepancy could be caused by current, steering error, leeway, etc.—you should think about
this. And always when beginning a new DR, use your latitude from your noon sight.

CONVERSION OF ARC TO TIME

0°–59°	h m	60°–119°	h m	120°–179°	h m	180°–239°	h m	240°–299°	h m	300°–359°	h m	′	0′.00 m s	0′.25 m s	0′.50 m s	0′.75 m s
0	0 00	60	4 00	120	8 00	180	12 00	240	16 00	300	20 00	0	0 00	0 01	0 02	0 03
1	0 04	61	4 04	121	8 04	181	12 04	241	16 04	301	20 04	1	0 04	0 05	0 06	0 07
2	0 08	62	4 08	122	8 08	182	12 08	242	16 08	302	20 08	2	0 08	0 09	0 10	0 11
3	0 12	63	4 12	123	8 12	183	12 12	243	16 12	303	20 12	3	0 12	0 13	0 14	0 15
4	0 16	64	4 16	124	8 16	184	12 16	244	16 16	304	20 16	4	0 16	0 17	0 18	0 19
5	0 20	65	4 20	125	8 20	185	12 20	245	16 20	305	20 20	5	0 20	0 21	0 22	0 23
6	0 24	66	4 24	126	8 24	186	12 24	246	16 24	306	20 24	6	0 24	0 25	0 26	0 27
7	0 28	67	4 28	127	8 28	187	12 28	247	16 28	307	20 28	7	0 28	0 29	0 30	0 31
8	0 32	68	4 32	128	8 32	188	12 32	248	16 32	308	20 32	8	0 32	0 33	0 34	0 35
9	0 36	69	4 36	129	8 36	189	12 36	249	16 36	309	20 36	9	0 36	0 37	0 38	0 39
10	0 40	70	4 40	130	8 40	190	12 40	250	16 40	310	20 40	10	0 40	0 41	0 42	0 43
11	0 44	71	4 44	131	8 44	191	12 44	251	16 44	311	20 44	11	0 44	0 45	0 46	0 47
12	0 48	72	4 48	132	8 48	192	12 48	252	16 48	312	20 48	12	0 48	0 49	0 50	0 51
13	0 52	73	4 52	133	8 52	193	12 52	253	16 52	313	20 52	13	0 52	0 53	0 54	0 55
14	0 56	74	4 56	134	8 56	194	12 56	254	16 56	314	20 56	14	0 56	0 57	0 58	0 59
15	1 00	75	5 00	135	9 00	195	13 00	255	17 00	315	21 00	15	1 00	1 01	1 02	1 03
16	1 04	76	5 04	136	9 04	196	13 04	256	17 04	316	21 04	16	1 04	1 05	1 06	1 07
17	1 08	77	5 08	137	9 08	197	13 08	257	17 08	317	21 08	17	1 08	1 09	1 10	1 11
18	1 12	78	5 12	138	9 12	198	13 12	258	17 12	318	21 12	18	1 12	1 13	1 14	1 15
19	1 16	79	5 16	139	9 16	199	13 16	259	17 16	319	21 16	19	1 16	1 17	1 18	1 19
20	1 20	80	5 20	140	9 20	200	13 20	260	17 20	320	21 20	20	1 20	1 21	1 22	1 23
21	1 24	81	5 24	141	9 24	201	13 24	261	17 24	321	21 24	21	1 24	1 25	1 26	1 27
22	1 28	82	5 28	142	9 28	202	13 28	262	17 28	322	21 28	22	1 28	1 29	1 30	1 31
23	1 32	83	5 32	143	9 32	203	13 32	263	17 32	323	21 32	23	1 32	1 33	1 34	1 35
24	1 36	84	5 36	144	9 36	204	13 36	264	17 36	324	21 36	24	1 36	1 37	1 38	1 39
25	1 40	85	5 40	145	9 40	205	13 40	265	17 40	325	21 40	25	1 40	1 41	1 42	1 43
26	1 44	86	5 44	146	9 44	206	13 44	266	17 44	326	21 44	26	1 44	1 45	1 46	1 47
27	1 48	87	5 48	147	9 48	207	13 48	267	17 48	327	21 48	27	1 48	1 49	1 50	1 51
28	1 52	88	5 52	148	9 52	208	13 52	268	17 52	328	21 52	28	1 52	1 53	1 54	1 55
29	1 56	89	5 56	149	9 56	209	13 56	269	17 56	329	21 56	29	1 56	1 57	1 58	1 59
30	2 00	90	6 00	150	10 00	210	14 00	270	18 00	330	22 00	30	2 00	2 01	2 02	2 03
31	2 04	91	6 04	151	10 04	211	14 04	271	18 04	331	22 04	31	2 04	2 05	2 06	2 07
32	2 08	92	6 08	152	10 08	212	14 08	272	18 08	332	22 08	32	2 08	2 09	2 10	2 11
33	2 12	93	6 12	153	10 12	213	14 12	273	18 12	333	22 12	33	2 12	2 13	2 14	2 15
34	2 16	94	6 16	154	10 16	214	14 16	274	18 16	334	22 16	34	2 16	2 17	2 18	2 19
35	2 20	95	6 20	155	10 20	215	14 20	275	18 20	335	22 20	35	2 20	2 21	2 22	2 23
36	2 24	96	6 24	156	10 24	216	14 24	276	18 24	336	22 24	36	2 24	2 25	2 26	2 27
37	2 28	97	6 28	157	10 28	217	14 28	277	18 28	337	22 28	37	2 28	2 29	2 30	2 31
38	2 32	98	6 32	158	10 32	218	14 32	278	18 32	338	22 32	38	2 32	2 33	2 34	2 35
39	2 36	99	6 36	159	10 36	219	14 36	279	18 36	339	22 36	39	2 36	2 37	2 38	2 39
40	2 40	100	6 40	160	10 40	220	14 40	280	18 40	340	22 40	40	2 40	2 41	2 42	2 43
41	2 44	101	6 44	161	10 44	221	14 44	281	18 44	341	22 44	41	2 44	2 45	2 46	2 47
42	2 48	102	6 48	162	10 48	222	14 48	282	18 48	342	22 48	42	2 48	2 49	2 50	2 51
43	2 52	103	6 52	163	10 52	223	14 52	283	18 52	343	22 52	43	2 52	2 53	2 54	2 55
44	2 56	104	6 56	164	10 56	224	14 56	284	18 56	344	22 56	44	2 56	2 57	2 58	2 59
45	3 00	105	7 00	165	11 00	225	15 00	285	19 00	345	23 00	45	3 00	3 01	3 02	3 03
46	3 04	106	7 04	166	11 04	226	15 04	286	19 04	346	23 04	46	3 04	3 05	3 06	3 07
47	3 08	107	7 08	167	11 08	227	15 08	287	19 08	347	23 08	47	3 08	3 09	3 10	3 11
48	3 12	108	7 12	168	11 12	228	15 12	288	19 12	348	23 12	48	3 12	3 13	3 14	3 15
49	3 16	109	7 16	169	11 16	229	15 16	289	19 16	349	23 16	49	3 16	3 17	3 18	3 19
50	3 20	110	7 20	170	11 20	230	15 20	290	19 20	350	23 20	50	3 20	3 21	3 22	3 23
51	3 24	111	7 24	171	11 24	231	15 24	291	19 24	351	23 24	51	3 24	3 25	3 26	3 27
52	3 28	112	7 28	172	11 28	232	15 28	292	19 28	352	23 28	52	3 28	3 29	3 30	3 31
53	3 32	113	7 32	173	11 32	233	15 32	293	19 32	353	23 32	53	3 32	3 33	3 34	3 35
54	3 36	114	7 36	174	11 36	234	15 36	294	19 36	354	23 36	54	3 36	3 37	3 38	3 39
55	3 40	115	7 40	175	11 40	235	15 40	295	19 40	355	23 40	55	3 40	3 41	3 42	3 43
56	3 44	116	7 44	176	11 44	236	15 44	296	19 44	356	23 44	56	3 44	3 45	3 46	3 47
57	3 48	117	7 48	177	11 48	237	15 48	297	19 48	357	23 48	57	3 48	3 49	3 50	3 51
58	3 52	118	7 52	178	11 52	238	15 52	298	19 52	358	23 52	58	3 52	3 53	3 54	3 55
59	3 56	119	7 56	179	11 56	239	15 56	299	19 56	359	23 56	59	3 56	3 57	3 58	3 59

The above table is for converting expressions in arc to their equivalent in time; its main use in this Almanac is for the conversion of longitude for application to LMT (*added* if *west*, *subtracted* if *east*) to give UT or vice versa, particularly in the case of sunrise, sunset, etc.

i

Formula for Noon Sight

To calculate latitude the following formula is used:

$$\text{Latitude} = 90° - \text{HO} = \text{ZD}$$
$$\text{ZD} +/- \text{Dec} = \text{Lat}$$

The advantage of local apparent noon sight is that it is only dependent on the observer's latitude and the declination of the sun. There is no GHA involved.

As the GP of the sun approaches the observer's meridian, the GHA of the sun becomes the longitude of the observer, thus the difference between the two is 0°. This is actually one definition of a meridian passage, when LHA = 0°. The sun will be bearing either due north or south on the observer's meridian. We have already shown that in celestial navigation, plotting that the LOP is perpendicular to the azimuth. So if you have an azimuth of either true north (0°) or true south (180°), then a line perpendicular to that is a 90° line, which on the earth is a parallel of latitude.

An aside: It could be said that the highest form of navigation at sea is actually deduced reckoning. For a mariner to completely understand his or her vessel on all points of sail, he or she needs to know: how much leeway the boat is making to windward; how steering error or the skill of steering keeps the boat on the desired heading; how the current affects the boat as it moves through the water; in other words, to be able to go from point A to point B with confidence. Without any tools at all, celestial navigation is actually the method used at sea to find out how good your dead reckoning is. By plotting position lines and accurately finding where you are in relation to the sun, you can then determine the error in your dead reckoning position. This is a goal that is hardly ever achieved, though there are experts who can navigate successfully without any sextant. The Pacific Islanders are well known for sailing long distances by using wave trains, the rising and setting of the stars to find their landfalls. Although Columbus is best remembered as an explorer, as a mariner his great achievement was that he sailed back and forth across to the New World basically using only dead reckoning. All he had was a primitive compass, no timepiece other than a half-hour sand timer, and an astrolabe. He had some primitive version of a chip log and yet four times he was able to get to Hispaniola and back to Spain again. No mean feat.

The Fix is in Plotting

Once you have done the book work and found the intercept, you are ready to turn these abstract numbers into a drawing. For me, this is the payoff for having to go through all the numbers in the tables. Those numbers mean nothing until they are drawn as lines that are easy to understand. The conversion of numbers to line drawings on the plotting sheet makes all the effort worthwhile. As an old teacher of mine used to say, "Plotting is an art experience." We are now drawing and should think of drawing a plotting sheet as "art." But don't be intimidated; you do not have to be a Picasso to effect gratifying results. If you can draw a straight line, you're golden.

The plotting sheets are called "universal plotting sheets" and come two to a page, one on either side, and are available from Celestaire (www.celestaire.com). They never go out of date and are user friendly once you understand them.

Look at the plotting sheet. There are parallel lines that will correspond to latitude. At the center is a large compass rose with the 0 pointing up. The numbers of the inside of the rose are what we are interested in. They increase numerically from the 0 to the right, replicating a compass. On the bottom right-hand side is a funny-looking drawing that resembles a misshapen segment of an ellipse. It is shorter at the top than at the bottom. On the right side, there is a degree number scale descending from 70° to 0°. On the bottom of the drawing is a notice that says "longitude scale." The right side is marked "mid-latitude scale." The lines going across represent latitude and the vertical lines represent longitude.

Remember, lines of latitude are always parallel to the equator, but meridians of longitude are only parallel at the equator because the earth being oblate spheroid, the meridians of longitude get closer together as they approach the poles. The plotting sheets are laid out as a Mercator Projection to accommodate this.

The advantage of plotting sheets is that they are inexpensive when compared to the price of paper charts. One could actually plot directly on the chart, but the custom is to replicate a small area of the chart, plot the LOP, and then put the EP on the chart. This way you minimize having lines all over an expensive chart. Look at the plotting sheet as a small segment of the chart that we are specifically relating to. In essence, we are making our own chart. The first thing we do is create the area you are concerned with. For example, let's say that the DR is N 40° 20' by W 72°30'.

First, go to the mid-latitude scale at the bottom of the chart and see a line going east-west marked 40°. Carefully, with a divider, mark that line from beginning to end with a pencil. This becomes our reference point.

Now take your dividers and extend them so that each leg touches the beginning and end of a line. Once you have done that, go to the compass rose and place one leg of the divider on the center of the rose and the other along the latitude line and make a mark. Go to the bottom of the rose and repeat. While the compass point is in the center, swing it to the other side so that you can make lines on the other side and then connect the dots. What we are doing is drawing meridians of longitude at our DR latitude. We label the mid-latitude line on the chart at 40°, and the one above at 41°, and the one below at 39°. I always use the center latitude line as my starting point, but there is nothing wrong with labeling the top line 40 and the mid-line 39, etc. Remember, we are recreating a chart and latitude that is equidistant from the equator to the poles, so it doesn't matter what we label the parallels of latitude. The vertical lines mark the meridians of longitude at 40° N. We know the shape of the earth that meridians of longitude converge as they get to the poles. So what our drawing represents is a Mercator Projection of a place anywhere on Earth at 40° N latitude. For the sake of convenience, I mark the center meridian at 72°, making the one to the right 71° and the one to the left 73°.

Now let's put our DR position at 40°20' by W 72°30'. Put one leg of the divider on the 40°20' latitude line. Next you want W 72°30'. You don't have to put the coordinates on the chart, just the symbol, which is universally understood. The next thing we want to do is plot our Assumed Position (AP). We know that the latitude is a whole number of degrees. Let's say for the sake of this exercise, the AP is N 40° by W 72°30'. We go down to the bottom of the diagram of the mid-latitude/longitude scale and place one leg of the dividers on our latitude of 40° where it intersects the curved line marked 30' and then we put the other leg on 0°.

We take the divider and put one leg of the divider to the left and make a mark and label this AP. One thing about drawing the AP: because entering arguments for HO249 always call for the creation of an Assumed Position based on a number for the whole degrees of latitude, no minutes or tenths, it will always be on a line of latitude. So we now look at our numbers from HO249. For this example, it says that the intercept was 7 miles toward with a bearing or Zn of 50°. So we want to see where we actually were when we took our sight. We know that our DR is just an educated guess. We need to see exactly where we are, so here's what we do.

Taking our dividers, we start at the center of the compass rose and place the dividers on the 50° mark on the inside of the compass rose. Then, walk one leg until we arrive at the AP, and then from the AP we draw a line.

Make it long and at the end place an arrowhead. This line is essential, as it is our bearing line and points to the direction or bearing of the sun. As you become more seasoned, you can eliminate this line. But for the time being it is of great value to have it on the chart in order to make our understanding easier. Our intercept is 7 nautical miles toward the GP of the sun and that means that from our AP we are 7 nautical miles toward the nautical object at a bearing of 50°.

We know that we always measure distance on a chart with a latitude scale, so we go to the center meridian line of the compass rose that is labeled 0 to 60° and with our dividers on the center point extend to 7. This is 7 nautical miles as measured on the latitude scale.

Make a mark on the bearing line and place your dividers on the line, then move it and place a right triangle on the bearing line so that it is perpendicular. As you'll recall, the LOP is always perpendicular to the bearing line. Then we scribe off the line.

The line extends and that is our LOP. We label it as such—and voilà—you are done.

Let's review what we've just done. The plotting sheet is constructed for the small area we are concerned with. The parallels of latitude can be labeled for the area we are dealing with. Parallels of latitude are always equidistant. Using the diagram at the bottom of the page labelled as mid-lati-

III. Example of Plot Basic

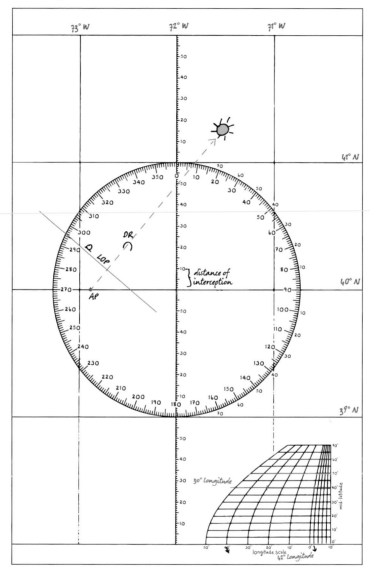

Basic Plot.

DR N 40°20 x W 72°30'
AP N 40° x 72°42'
Intercept 10 NM toward Zn 040°

S 60	16 27	17 11	18 00	22 22	23 31	24 40	00 40
	SUN			MOON			
Day	Eqn. of Time		Mer.	Mer. Pass.		Age	Phase
	00^h	12^h	Pass.	Upper	Lower		
d	m s	m s	h m	h m	h m	d	%
25	01 54	01 59	11 58	18 01	05 37	07	45
26	02 04	02 09	11 58	18 47	06 24	08	55
27	02 14	02 19	11 58	19 31	07 09	09	64

Noon sight, April 27

tude/longitude scale we mark off the distance each meridian of longitude is at our specific DR latitude. Lay out the plotting sheet and mark DR and AP. You will always be plotting from the AP. Draw a bearing line to the celestial object then mark off the intercept on that line. Then mark off the intercept either toward or away from the celestial object, using the latitude scale on the chart to mark distance. Then draw a Line of Position at right angles to the bearing line. Label it and then create an EP from which we begin our new DR position and plot the next sight from there. This will all become obvious once you have practiced.

Now, we have established the basics and if you are interested enough, you will practice and all that has been written will become clearer. I hope I have succeeded in whetting your interest.

Step-by-Step Sight Reduction

A. Sextant Sight Correction Sequence

Overview: The reading from the sextant (Hs) needs to be corrected for index error, height of eye, and the third sun correction to give Ho, the observed altitude.

1. Find Hs, the angle that you read off of your sextant.
2. Apply the index correction, if there is an error.
3. Correct for the height of eye using the dip table on the inside front cover of the *Nautical Almanac*. The dip correction is always subtracted. The result is the apparent altitude, or Ha.
4. Determine and apply the third correction from the inside front cover of the *Nautical Almanac*.
5. The final result is Ho, the observed altitude.

B. Using the *Nautical Almanac*

Overview: The *Nautical Almanac* is used to pinpoint the declination and GHA of the sun (or other celestial body) second by second. Enter the daily pages with the Greenwich Mean Time (GMT) of the sight, GHA, and declination.

1. Find the page in the *Nautical Almanac* with the date of your sight.
2. On the left side of the right page is a column with every hour of the three days covered on that page. Go down the column until you find the correct hour in GMT of the correct day.
3. Find the GHA and the declination of the sun in the next two columns and extract those numbers.

4. At the bottom of the declination column is a value for d. If the declination is decreasing during the day, then d is negative; if declination is increasing, then d is positive.

5. At the back of the *Nautical Almanac* is a section labeled "Increments and Corrections." There is half a page for each minute. Find the page with the correct minute of GMT. Move down the far left column to row for seconds of GMT. On that row, move to first column to right (for sun and planets). Add this number to the GHA for the final GHA.

6. Staying in the same box, there is a column labeled "v" or d. Go down that column until you find your value for d. The number directly to its right should be added to the declination if d is positive and subtracted if d is negative.

C. Find the LHA & Assumed Latitude

Overview: LHA is the combination of GHA and the assumed longitude. In the Western Hemisphere LHA = GHA - assumed longitude. In the Eastern Hemisphere LHA = GHA + assumed longitude.

1. To enter the tables, LHA must always be to whole degrees, and have no minutes or no tenths. In the Western Hemisphere the minutes of the assumed longitude always equal the minutes of the GHA. Assumed longitude is not the same as DR longitude.

2. Start with GHA and then fill in the minutes of assumed longitude so that the minutes of LHA = 0.

Make the degrees of the assumed longitude as close as possible to the DR longitude.

3. To find assumed latitude, take the DR latitude and round it off to the nearest degree.

Step-by-Step Sight Reduction

D. HO249

Overview: The sight reduction tables are based on a set of algorithms derived from the navigational triangle. They convert the assumed latitude, declination, and LHA into Zn and a calculated altitude (Hc). It is a calculated altitude because it is based on the Assumed Position.

1. Enter the table with assumed latitude, declination, LHA.
2. Find the correct page:
   a. First, find a page with your assumed latitude.
   b. Second, find a page with the degrees of declination (0–14) or (15–29).
   c. Third, determine if the declination and latitude are the same or contrary. (They are the same if both are north or both are south; contrary if one is north and one is south.)
   d. Fourth, find the page with the proper same or contrary designation.
   e. Fifth, recheck to make sure that the page has the proper latitude, declination, and sign.

3. Find the correct column for degrees of declination. Find the correct row with LHA running up and down the sides of the page. LHA is greater than 180° on the right side of the page and less than 180° on the left side. It sometimes runs over to the next page.
4. Extract Hc, d, and Z; make sure to get the proper sign for d; the sign is not printed on each row.
5. Convert Z to Zn (azimuth) using these formulas supplied on each page:

Northern Hemisphere: Southern Hemisphere:
LHA > 180 then Zn = Z   LHA > 180 then Zn = 180 - Z
LHA < 180 then Zn = 360 - Z   LHA < 180 then Zn = 180 + Z

6. Use Table 5 in back of volume: enter with d and minutes of declination. If d is positive, add result to Hc; if d is negative, subtract result from Hc. This gives the final value of Hc.

E. Find the Intercept

Overview: This is determining whether our position is closer to the sun than the Assumed Position. The larger the altitude, the closer to the sun.

1. Find the difference between Hc and Ho (subtract one from the other). Each minute equals a nautical mile.
2. Determine if the intercept is to be plotted toward or away. If Hc is greater than Ho, plot away; if Hc is less than Ho, plot toward.

F. Plotting

Overview: The plotting sheet should be used for keeping a DR track as well as for celestial information. For a sun sight use the assumed latitude, assumed longitude, Zn, and intercept to create a Line of Position (LOP). Remember, one sight yields one LOP, not a fix.

1. Set up your plotting sheet for your area of the ocean.
2. Plot your Assumed Position (AP). Assumed latitude is the whole degree of latitude used to enter HO249. Assumed longitude is the longitude subtracted from GHA to get LHA, not your DR longitude.
3. Plot your Zn (azimuth). The azimuth direction needs to be plotted through the Assumed Position and then draw an arrow on the end of that line in the direction of the sun (i.e., if the azimuth = 129°, then on the end that points toward 129°).
4. Plot the intercept. Starting at the Assumed Position (AP) plot toward or away from the sun along the azimuth line and mark.
5. Plot the LOP. The LOP must be perpendicular to the azimuth. Add or subtract 90° to/from the azimuth. Plot this line through the intercept. Label one end with "Sun" over the line and the time underneath it.

Used by permission of *Ocean Navigator* magazine.

A Parting Word

I appreciate your patience and hope that I have clearly explained the protocol for using the sun to find position. I have no doubt that many of you will be frustrated by my efforts, but persist in your studies. I have tried not to make this a textbook, for very few of us have either the time or inclination to read textbooks. I do think that if you look over this little guide, buy a sextant, some copies of HO249 and an up-to-date *Nautical Almanac*, and practice a bit that much of the information will become clear.

Thanks for coming along with me and I hope this adds some value to your lives.

—Dave Berson, April 2018

Sources of Information

The American Practical Navigator by Nathaniel Bowditch
Chapman Piloting and Seamanship
Celestial Navigation for Yachtsmen by Mary Blewett
Sextant Handbook by Bruce Bauer
Primer of Navigation by George W. Mixter
Coming of Age in the Milky Way by Timothy Ferris
The Discoverers by Daniel J. Boorstin
Celestial Navigation by David Burch and Tobias Burch
Practical Celestial Navigation by Susan P. Howell
Sky and Sextant by John B. Budlong

Definitions

Altitude: Angular distance of the celestial body above the observer's horizon.

Altitude, apparent (Ha): Value after Hs has been corrected for index error and dip.

Altitude, calculated (Hc): Value for altitude from the tables or calculator based on an Assumed Position. Found in the sight reduction tables.

Altitude, observed (Ho): Value for altitude after all sight corrections have been applied to sextant altitude (Hs).

Altitude, sextant (Hs): Value read directly from the sextant before any corrections have been applied.

Apparent altitude correction: Also known as third correction including semi-diameter, refraction, and parallax.

Applied to Hs to find Ho. The tables for this correction are found on the inside cover of the *Nautical Almanac*.

Assumed latitude: Usually the whole value of the DR position, with no minutes or tenths, used to enter the sight reduction tables. Used to plot the Assumed Position.

Assumed longitude: In the Western Hemisphere, the longitude is subtracted from the GHA to give a value of LHA in whole number of degrees, with no minutes or tenths. In the Eastern Hemisphere, the assumed longitude is added to the GHA to give LHA. Basis for plotting the Assumed Position.

Assumed Position (AP): A position used as the starting point for plotting an LOP. The Assumed Position is defined by the assumed latitude and assumed longitude. Based on the DR position and entered in sight reduction tables as whole number of degrees, no minutes or tenths.

Azimuth (Zn): The bearing in true degrees from the observer to the sun. What we are solving for in the sight reduction tables.

Azimuth angle (Z): The angle in the navigational triangle at the observer's zenith. In the Northern Hemisphere, Z = Zn if LHA > 180°; if LHA < 180° then Zn = 360° - Z. Instructions are given on every page of the sight reduction tables in the upper left-hand corner.

Bearing: The direction from the observer to an object. Measured using a compass rose with north = 0°, east = 90°, south = 180°, and west = 270°.

Celestial equator: 0° of declination on the celestial sphere. It is the projection of the earth's equator on the imaginary celestial sphere.

Celestial sphere: The imaginary projection of all celestial bodies on the inside of a sphere at an infinite distance with the earth as its center.

d: An interpolation factor. There are two different d's used in a typical sight reduction. The first is found at the bottom of the declination column on the daily page of the *Nautical Almanac.* It is taken to the increments and correction pages in the back of the almanac to determine the d correction, which is applied to the declination. The other d is found in the body of HO249. It is taken to Table 5 in the back of HO249 to find a correction, which is applied to Hc.

Dead reckoning (DR): A position or method of finding a position using only speed and course steered from a known position.

Declination (dec): The measure of a body's position north or south of the celestial equator. Analogous to latitude on Earth.

Dip: The height of eye correction applied to Hs. Found in the dip table on the inside front cover of the *Nautical Almanac.*

Ecliptic: The apparent path of the sun around the celestial sphere in the course of a year.

Estimated position (EP): A more accurate position than a DR based on the LOP. Found by dropping a perpendicular from the LOP to the DR (the shortest distance). The EP is placed where this perpendicular crosses the LOP. It is the beginning of a new plot on the chart.

Fix: The intersection of two or more LOPs.

GHA (Greenwich Hour Angle): The angular measure of a body's position west of the Greenwich meridian, which is Greenwich Hour Angle, or 0°. Similar to longitude on Earth, except that it is only measured west through 360°.

GMT (Greenwich Mean Time): The mean time at 0° longitude at the Greenwich meridian. This is the time used within the *Nautical Almanac*. Also called Universal Time (UT). All celestial navigation observations use GMT.

GP (Geographic Position): The point on Earth directly under the celestial body if the object is defined by its declination and GHA, which can be converted to latitude and longitude on the surface of the earth.

HO249: Sight reduction tables. Vol II and Vol III used for all bodies with a declination of less than 30°. Easiest to use for most navigators.

Index error: A sextant error resulting from the misalignment of the horizon glass. This should be determined before each sight and corrected for during the sight correction process. If the error is off the arc, the correction is added; if the error is on the arc, the correction is subtracted. Remember the mnemonic "if you are on you are off, if you are off you are on."

Intercept: The distance from the Assumed Position to the LOP measured along the Zn. This is determined by finding the difference between Hc and Ho. It is plotted toward the direction of Zn. If Ho is greater than Hc, remember Ho Mo toward, which indicates that the intercept written in nautical miles is closer to the GP of the sun. If Ho is less than the Hc intercept is plotted away from the GP.

LAN (Local Apparent Noon): The time when the sun's azimuth is directly north or south of the observer. In other words, when the sun is on the meridian of the observer. The angular height of the sun is the highest at this moment.

Latitude: Parallels measuring north and south from the equator on Earth, from 0° at the equator to 90°. Always written either N or S. Custom has it that latitude is written before longitude as N x° by W y°. Used to measure distance on the chart. One minute of latitude is one nautical mile.

LHA (Local Hour Angle): The angular measurement west from the observer's longitude to the GP of the body. In the Western Hemisphere, subtract longitude from GHA; in the Eastern Hemipshere, add the two. LHA is used to enter HO249 and must have full degrees, no minutes or tenths.

Longitude: Meridians of longitude measure east and west from the Greenwich meridian to 180°. Never used for measuring distance on the chart. Always written as either east or west.

LOP (Line of Position): A small segment of a Circle of Position. Drawn through the intercept perpendicular to the Zn.

Lower limb: Bottom of the edge of the sun. Preferred limb to observe with the sextant when taking an observation. Limb will "kiss" the horizon (the sun or the moon).

Nautical mile: One minute of latitude. It is about 6,076 feet long.

Nautical twilight: The time in the morning or evening when the sun is 12° below the horizon.

Navigational triangle: A spherical triangle formed on the celestial sphere by a celestial pole, the AP of the observer, and the GP of the sun.

Running fix (RFIX): The intersection of an LOP and another LOP that has been advanced along a DR track.

Upper limb: The top edge of the sun. Used not as frequently as the lower limb, but valid if one is comfortable with bringing the sun up to the horizon instead of lowering it onto the horizon.

Zenith: The point on the celestial sphere directly over the observer. Location if the observer was exactly underneath the celestial flagpole looking up.